MEMOIRS OF DESMOND FITZGERALD

Memoirs of
Desmond FitzGerald

1913 — 1916

London

Routledge & Kegan Paul

First published 1968
by Routledge and Kegan Paul Ltd
Broadway House, 68–74 Carter Lane
London E.C.4

Printed in Great Britain
by Western Printing Services Limited
Bristol.

SBN 7100 2878 4

Contents

	List of Plates	*vi*
	Editors' introduction	*page vii*
Chapter one	Introduction	*1*
Chapter two	Early days in Kerry	*6*
Chapter three	The Volunteer Movement	*25*
Chapter four	The Split in the Volunteers	*53*
Chapter five	Expelled to Wicklow	*67*
Chapter six	Arrest, trial and imprisonment	*84*
Chapter seven	Preparation for the Rising	*107*
Chapter eight	The G.P.O.	*131*
Chapter nine	Escape and return home	*160*
Appendix	Shaw letters	*181*
	Index	*199*

List of Plates

facing page

1. Desmond Fitzgerald (*c. 1922*)   98

2. Desmond Fitzgerald at a Celtic Congress in the early '20's. (*Photo: Topical Press Agency*).   99

3. Arthur Griffith and Desmond Fitzgerald, 1921. (*Photo: Radio Times Hulton Picture Library*).   114

4. The General Post Office, Dublin, after the Easter rising. (*Photo: Independent Newspapers Limited*).   115

5. O'Connell Street, Dublin, at the time of the 1916 rising. (*Photo: Independent Newspapers Limited*).   115

6. Arthur Griffith. (*Photo: Irish Independent*).   146

7. Michael Collins, leaving the Treaty Debate in January 1922. (*Photo: Irish Independent*).   147

8. Liberty Hall, headquarters of the Citizen Army, after being shelled during the 1916 rising. (*Photo: Irish Independent*).   162

9. Arthur Griffith and Michael Collins. (*Photo: Irish Independent*).   163

Editors' Introduction

Urged by a number of friends, during the Second World War Desmond FitzGerald began to set down this account of events which had occurred thirty years earlier, before and during the Easter Rising of 1916. He had intended to continue the story at least up to the Anglo-Irish Treaty and the Irish Civil War which followed its ratification, but two difficulties made him delay completion and when he died in 1947 at the age of fifty-nine the unfinished manuscript did not reach beyond the week following the surrender by the leaders of the Irish Volunteers to the British forces in Dublin in 1916.

The first difficulty Desmond FitzGerald encountered in continuing the story was that he had no wish to write an autobiography in the normal sense. His friends had persuaded him, as a participant in the historical events which created an independent Ireland, to record what he knew of those events. Scrupulous about the truth, Desmond would not set down anything he had not personally taken part in or witnessed, and this limitation forced him to write in effect a personal account. Yet all the time he strove to avoid mention of himself in any but an objective way. This attempt to write an eyewitness account with the minimum of reference to the 'I' was one reason why he did not pursue his task with greater rapidity, for on other subjects he wrote easily and relatively quickly.

The second reason for his slow progress was that he did not

wish to write anything hurtful about people who could be identified. How hard he tried can be seen from the great lengths he went to in order to avoid mentioning those of whom he could not in all truthfulness speak with admiration. This second restriction made virtually impossible the writing of the later part of the work—the days of the First Dail, the Black-and-Tan war, the Treaty negotiations and especially the Civil War and its aftermath. Had he put it all down on paper in a first draft, he or others could have done the necessary pruning afterwards. But this he would not do for fear others might some day see this first draft and the criticisms or implied criticisms.

While these two self-imposed restrictions prevented the work from reaching the point in time originally planned, they do not detract from that part of the text which was completed, that is to say the story of the Insurrection of 1916. It is intriguing to note how, in line with the first of the two limitations, he makes the minimum of references to his wife, and when he is compelled to mention her he does so in the most detached manner possible. No clue is given to Mabel FitzGerald's role in the national movement. The appendix to the book containing the correspondence between Bernard Shaw and Mabel in 1914/1915 shows a glimpse of a very different side of the story.

Desmond FitzGerald was born and brought up in London, but he had visited County Kerry in his youth, whence his mother had emigrated, and he had a romantic love for that western brink of Europe. As a very young man he joined a group of equally young poets calling themselves the *Imagists*. This group included T. E. Hulme, F. S. Flint, Hilda Doolittle, Edward Storer, Richard Aldington, Harold Monro. They were all English with the exception of Desmond himself. Only later did Ezra Pound cross the Atlantic to join them for a short spell before moving on southwards. It was Desmond FitzGerald, with Florence Farr who introduced him to the group.*

.   .   .

* Patricia Hutchins, *Ezra Pound's Kensington*, p. 128.

At this stage in Desmond FitzGerald's life it would have been difficult to have forecast his later career—patriot, revolutionary soldier, convict, member of parliament, minister of state, Catholic philosopher. The young poets who drew their aesthetic values from Baudelaire, Verlaine, Rimbaud, Mallarmé and Verhaeren probably gave little serious thought to such issues as 'The Irish Question', and if Desmond did so at that time, it can have been with no foreboding of the road down which it would lead him.

In 1913 Desmond moved with his Northern Irish wife from France, where they had lived since their marriage a year or two earlier, to the most westerly peninsula of Kerry. It is at this point that his account begins.

The story set out in the following pages ends on 1st May, 1916 after Desmond's evacuation of the wounded from the General Post Office at the conclusion of the week's fighting in Dublin. He describes reaching his house in Bray by crossing the mountains from Dublin. There he remained for three days, until he was arrested and brought to Kilmainham gaol, court-martialled and sentenced to life imprisonment, later commuted to twenty years. Together with the other Irishmen who had been given long sentences, he was sent to Dartmoor and later moved to Maidstone in the south of England, handcuffed to Eamonn de Valera and Dr. Richard Hayes.

In 1918 Desmond FitzGerald was nominated Sinn Fein candidate for the traditionally Unionist constituency of Pembroke, which he won by a large margin. As Desmond was a convict in prison, the slogan was: 'Put him in to get him out!' It was indeed an embarrassment for the British government to have M.P.'s in convict prisons, and all those who were elected in the General Election at the end of 1918 were in fact released. They refused to attend Westminster and established their own parliament (Dail) in Dublin. The Dail set up its own government, with Eamonn de Valera as President of the Dail and in April 1919, Desmond FitzGerald was appointed Substitute Director of Publicity in place of Laurence Ginnell, who had been sent on a mission to South America. Through his literary friends in London he made contact with foreign journalists there, his reappearance on the London scene in this new role provoking Ezra Pound to write later of:

> The live man, out of lands and prisons, shakes the dry pods,
> Probes for old wills and friendships, and the big locust-casques,
> Bend to the tawdy table,
> Lift up spoons to mouths, put forks in cutlets,
> And make sound like the sound of voices★

Back in Ireland he provided the link between visiting foreign journalists and the Sinn Fein movement and edited the mimeo-graphed daily *Bulletin*, the underground news-sheet which was distributed to the world's newspapers to offset the official British accounts of the fighting in Ireland. However, in March 1921 Desmond was again arrested and his place as editor of the *Bulletin* was taken over temporarily by Erskine Childers.

He was released from prison for the Treaty negotiations, accompanying the Irish plenipotentiaries to London. He was, in fact, the person who carried the final text back to Dublin. In the twelve days of Dail debates on the Treaty he favoured its acceptance and supported Arthur Griffith, Michael Collins and the others who advocated a settlement with Britain on the basis of the terms negotiated in London.

As a result of the Treaty, the Irish Free State came into existence. Soon afterwards Desmond FitzGerald became Minister for External Affairs and on 17th April, 1923 he signed the letter of application of the Irish Free State for admission to the League of Nations. The Irish Free State was formally admitted on 10th September. He also represented Ireland at the Imperial Conferences of 1923, 1926 and 1930 and at the League of Nations during much of this period.

On a Sunday morning in July 1927, while Desmond Fitz-Gerald was ill in hospital the Minister for Justice, Kevin

★ Canto VII.

O'Higgins, was assassinated on his way to Mass. In the resulting Cabinet reshuffle Desmond FitzGerald was appointed Minister for Defence, which he held until the government was defeated at the General Election of 1932. Thereafter he served as Opposition Deputy and Senator, until 1943. He died in April 1947 at the age of 59.

Not all of those who took part in the combat for Irish freedom aroused Desmond's personal admiration. Those whom he admired were therefore all the more dear to him, and many of them died tragically within ten years of the Rising of 1916. The O'Rahilly, who was killed in the Rising, was one of these, Arthur Griffith, the founder of Sinn Fein, who died at the beginning of the Civil War after a life devoted to achieving Ireland's independence, was another. Others were Michael Collins, who was shot in an ambush near his home in West Cork a few days after Arthur Griffith's death; Kevin O'Higgins, Vice-Premier and Minister for Justice who was assassinated in 1927.

In spite of his busy and dangerous life during the years from 1916 to 1922, Desmond FitzGerald did not abandon his love of literature. An admirer of W. B. Yeats from boyhood, he now got to know him, as well as AE (George Russell), Joseph Campbell, Padraic Colum and others of the Anglo-Irish school of writing. In 1919 he had a short play—*The Saint*—produced in the Abbey Theatre in Dublin.

Later, in the early 1920s, he sought to associate the new State officially with literature by visiting James Joyce in Paris to propose that the Irish Free State should put his name forward for the Nobel Prize—a proposal which came to nothing however.*

At the same time he developed an interest in philosophy, extending his association with French writers from the poets to the philosophers, including Jacques Maritain, with whom he became especially friendly. In 1937 and 1938 he was invited by the University of Notre-Dame (Indiana) to give courses of

* Richard Elliman, *James Joyce*, p. 546.

lectures in the philosophy of politics, and in 1939 published a book on this subject, *Preface to Statecraft*.

Looking back on Desmond FitzGerald's early life, there would seem to be little there that foreshadowed his entry into the militant Irish separatist movement. But he had a deep romantic affection for Ireland, and his love of poetry had brought him early to admire the writings of W. B. Yeats and other Irish writers of that period. Reason rather than romance was, however, the moving force in his actions once he had chosen the path to follow. In his life of Kevin O'Higgins* Terence de Vere White speaks of Desmond FitzGerald as 'a man of extraordinary physical and moral courage'. Simone Tery† described his remarkable physical courage as a consequence of his moral courage based upon dignity and self-respect, while Joseph Kessel, a French journalist who visited Ireland in 1920‡ has given a more dramatic description of his 'fair hair, almost Venetian, floating around a high, unlined, forehead; his appearance was of a noble, ardent and daring delicateness; and in his light blue eyes shone simultaneously gaiety, tenderness, courage and poetry—a sort of inspired light-heartedness exuded from this magnificent youth'.

His wife, Mabel, who, by her own wish, is so rarely and impersonally referred to in Desmond's account, was romantically interested in Irish freedom. Her father was a Northern Unionist businessman. After graduating from Queens College, Belfast, Mabel went to London to take a post-graduate course in education at London University. She was a daughter of her time—as well as being an Irish Nationalist, she was also a strong believer in women's rights and a Fabian. To all that she undertook she gave her full enthusiasm and energy.

Hearing that Bernard Shaw required a temporary secretary, she wrote to him and he engaged her on the spot. She stayed with him for a while, leaving to make a round-the-world tour

* Terence de Vere White, *Kevin O'Higgins*, London, 1948
† Simone Tery, *En Irelande*, Paris, 1924.
‡ Joseph Kessel, *Temoin parmi les hommes*, Paris, 1956.

in the company of one of her brothers. Later she worked for a period for George Moore.

After her marriage to Desmond FitzGerald, they lived for a short while in France, and then in early 1913 went to live in Kerry. The second part of this book contains the surviving part of an exchange of correspondence she initiated with Shaw from Kerry shortly after the outbreak of the Great War. Reading it one finds that, in Shaw's mind, it was Mabel, the suffragette, socialist, and revolutionary, who had a large measure of responsibility for bringing Desmond into the national movement. This can have been only one of several motivating influences, but her intellectual enthusiasms carried considerable force. Mabel continued to be active in the struggle for independence during the year that followed 1916. She was appointed secretary to Cumann na mBan, the women's national organization. When the Treaty was debated in the Dail, Mabel, like most of the women in the movement, favoured continuing the fight rather than accepting a compromise. But she took no active part in the Civil War that followed, and never allowed her political differences with her husband to interfere with her marriage. In later life she came to feel that those who had favoured the Treaty had been right, and that the national ideals could best be achieved by the evolution of events on the basis of the Treaty.

Mabel died in Dublin eleven years after her husband. She had never thought of herself as other than a helpmeet to Desmond, and was quite unaware of her own contribution. She never put down on paper her own experiences, largely for the same reasons that prevented Desmond from completing his autobiography. She had a fund of anecdotes not merely about the national movement but about other events—some strangely removed from the interests one might have expected her to have—but these stories, like so many of Desmond's humorous tales, will never now be recorded.

F.FG.

CHAPTER ONE

Introduction

Somebody has said that we begin to write our memoirs when we begin to lose our memories. And certainly some degree of loss of memory, or a blurring of memory may well be helpful in writing memoirs. The process of forgetting is really a form of selection. One only remembers the things that are more 'interesting', or things that in themselves form some sort of unity.

Naturally I have forgotten many things completely, and there are other things that only recur to my mind when something specifically recalls them. At the same time I have generally found that I frequently remember things more clearly than do those who went through the same experiences with me. Consequently it may well be that though there will be some complete gaps in what I recall, at the same time I may have to make up for lack of forgetfulness by conscious selection. I may also digress considerably.

But these are not the only disadvantages of memory for writing reminiscences. Although 'reminiscing' is by nature an egocentric form of writing it has necessarily to refer to other people. And here a blurring of memory would be very useful. For while when we know a person intimately we are aware of the many-sidedness of his character, of the contradictions in his nature, with the process of time we may forget so much that we may remember only some outstanding characteristic, his personal charm, his nobility or his meanness. And our conscience is easy that in presenting him in such a light we show him as he really was. While when the memory is clear, we feel that everything we affirm about him, every aspect of him that we show, is misleading unless we give further information that will modify the impression that we have conveyed. The result is that he must appear very unconvincing, and much less real than if he were depicted in the firm lines of one characteristic. And when one writes of a man who was known to the public one has to bear in mind that the public have already judged him and placed him in a category, and will repudiate anything that seems to jeopardize the position that has been allotted to him. And the public will hardly accept it as a valid excuse that a personal reminiscence is merely what one person remembers.

With that much stated we may as well move towards the memories. I cannot set out to catalogue the forces that directed the generation of Irishmen to which I belong to move along the path we chose, but it is pretty certain that Mr. Arthur Griffith was the greatest influence. The little paper he edited had a very restricted sale. The smallness of its circulation might well have led people to assume that it was not likely to have any effect in the country, for people always think that influence must be direct and visible. Whereas in the realm of ideas it is more frequently indirect and occult. You may talk to a peasant in the West of Ireland about political ideas and come away convinced that he is steeped in Rousseauism. But you must not assume that he has read Rousseau. On the contrary he has never met anybody who had heard of Rousseau. And yet he presupposes many things that he might never have dreamed of if Rousseau had not written. Again you may be talking to a young person in a country town, and when she remarks that she has a terrible fixation on so-and-so, but is afflicted with an awful inferiority complex, you may, if you are sufficiently foolish, think that on her book-shelves you would find well-thumbed copies of Freud. But as a matter of fact, not only has she never seen a work written by Freud, but she has never known anybody who has seen such a work. And yet at the same time it is clear from the fact that she uses the Freudian vocabulary that her conception of human nature has been affected by Freud's theories.

In the same way, people who thought that Arthur Griffith only affected the minute circle who read his paper were gravely in error. One meeting addressed by a parliamentary leader might contain three times as many people as bought Griffith's paper. The speeches delivered at that meeting and the speeches delivered in the Westminster Parliament were published in all the daily papers. Those same daily papers gave leading articles dealing with the points in those speeches. And while that was happening it usually happened if you went into a newsagent's in a small town and asked for Griffith's paper, the reply was that they did not stock it, or that they only had a certain number for people who ordered it. But if you moved on from there to some place where people were gathered together to talk and argue you would find somebody giving voice to Griffith's teaching, or even quoting him by name.

Of course he was not the only influence on our generation. There were many others. There was the Gaelic League which set out to get people to talk Irish, and if it did not get them to do that, at least it induced a number of people to talk about the language, and that implied a certain national self-consciousness. In 1898 there had been the Centenary of the 1798 Rebellion. The supplements that were published that year by newspapers were still to be found in houses where there was very little other reading matter. There was the Anglo-Irish literary movement led by W. B. Yeats which influenced a certain select circle. If one made an elaborate examination one would probably find an enormous number of small streams that flowed into our generation, some of them only influencing a select few. The truth is that there was a national tradition, possibly not very clearly defined, which was given an additional reality and significance by the work of Griffith, who as it were correlated the past with the present, interpreted the facts of history in relation to the actualities of his time, and read a national moral into everything that he commented upon.

In any case, my own experience was that whenever you met a man who was more than usually earnest in his love of Ireland you would find that he was to a greater or less degree a follower of Arthur Griffith.

My own first discovery of Sinn Fein was through Mr. Griffith's policy. I suppose I was already ashamed and indignant that the representatives of my country should have been pleading for decades to deaf ears in the House of Commons for a minimum concession. And those representatives seemed at that stage of history to look upon the concession of Home Rule as something that would satisfy our national aspirations to the full. I think that reading only a few of Griffith's articles revealed to me the nobility of his character (and how noble he was!). In any case I soon was satisfied that Griffith was a natural leader of our people, and became his devoted disciple.

He had had the same effect upon many others but they were a small minority of the whole people. But his effect upon the country cannot be measured by the mere number of those who directly supported him. It is certain that his teaching touched many who still gave support to the Home Rule party. There were always grounds for believing that in spite of all previous disappointments Home Rule was about to become a reality. One might just as well give it another chance. If Home Rule did become a fact it would certainly make it easier to move on to that larger freedom that Griffith and his followers demanded. And if it did not, even with that last chance, well, it would be time enough then to see what the new policy could achieve.

I imagine that when 1913 was reached the position was that Griffith had a smallish minority (mostly young men) who were enthusiastic followers, while a fairly large number of the people who supported Mr. Redmond's Party were inclined to be critical and possibly cynical. If Home Rule came quickly, well and good. No doubt it could be used beneficially as a point from which we could evolve nationally. But if it did not come soon, then it would be time to try something else.

CHAPTER TWO

Early days in Kerry

In the early part of 1913 I was living abroad. But in 1910 I had spent some time on the Blaskets. I do not know what there was about that Island or its people or the life they lived that made such a powerful appeal to me, but I do know that when I left it I felt that I must at all cost get back there or at least within sight of it. At that time there had been very few visitors to the Island. The outer world had hardly intruded upon its traditional life. The years that have intervened since then have certainly brought great changes there.* In spite of that, I think that the instantaneous success of 'Twenty Years a Growing' owes something to the fact that that book coming from that Island gives some reflection of whatever it was that stirred me so deeply. But as I have said at that time the traditional had suffered much less change than is the case now. The old men that I knew are probably nearly all dead. Few of them had been to a national school and they did not read newspapers. But they loved to talk and to argue. And when the small events of the day were exhausted what could they turn to but the traditions that they had learned from their fathers before them. That does not mean that they were a simple, gullible people. Far from it. They described to me all the foibles of previous

* *Ed. note:* At the time this was written the Island was still inhabited, but it is now deserted.

visitors to the Island. And when some of their own relatives came back from America on a visit, and tried to impress the natives, the islanders were not impressed. Stories of the Elevated Railway, of the Subway, of the enormous cities and the traffic on the streets, were listened to politely, but with a certain amount of pity for the poor soul who expected them to be impressed by that sort of thing. The affectations acquired in America were noted with amusement. The habit of these returned 'exiles' of interlarding their conversation with the explanatory remark, 'Mar a dheinimid sall' (as we do over there, i.e. in the United States) was apparently so general that that phrase was used as a name for them. It often happened that when I came back from a walk to the far end of the Island I would meet a man looking for a returned American who happened to be there at that time. 'An bhfaca tu "Mar a dheinimid sall" in aon ait?' (Did you see 'As we do over there anywhere'?) he would ask.

When I had been on the island for some time another visitor arrived, a lady from Dublin. She was a vegetarian who brought her own special nut food with her. She also brought her stretcher bed and she wore sandals. Of course she was a theosophist. She spoke Irish with a high English voice. The islanders should certainly have appreciated her for all the amusement she gave them. I often watched them as they struggled to keep from laughing as she held forth to them. If they caught my eye, they would inevitably burst out laughing, and then try to cover it up by coming to me with the words, 'Era, nach duine macanta thu, Gearailtaigh' (Yerra, aren't you the decent man Mr. FitzGerald). But they all had the idea that she was tormenting me. When she arrived she had told me to put up her stretcher bed in the King's room. (I don't know if she made any enquiries as to where he, poor man was to sleep). But after a little experience of that room she declared that it was damp. I may say that the day she arrived I had offered to give her the guest room that I occupied. That had been arranged as soon as we heard that she was coming, and I agreed to it very readily, as it would mean that I should go to stay with Tomas O Criomhthain, the most interesting talker on the Island. But she had refused to allow me to be disturbed. When she discovered that the King's room was damp, I had to put up her bed in the kitchen. But again this turned out to be unsatisfactory, as it was the custom of the men to foregather in that room every morning early before they went out fishing. And it never occurred to them that she might object to waking up at six in the morning and finding them all there. Then she decided to take the guest room from me. If she had done that when she arrived it would have suited me splendidly, but now if I went to O Criomhthain's house, it would make trouble as it would be thought that I had been driven out of the King's house by her. I had therefore to accept the King's damp room for a while, until I left. The King was convinced that she was the cause of my leaving. The day before I went he had got half a barrel of porter over from the mainland and he constantly tried to make amends by inviting me to have a drink. And when I refused he drank it himself. In the evening he called me outside and made a little speech to me in English in a stage whisper. 'Mr. Fitz-Gerald' he said, 'I had Mr. Synge here, a very nize gentleman. And I had Carl Marstrander here, a very nize gentleman. And I had Professor MacAlister here, a very nize gentleman. And you Mr. FitzGerald, you are a very nize gentleman.' And then in a lower whisper still, 'De men is all right, but de vimmen is de divil.' I realized that this was an explanation and an apology, but I could hardly convey to him the fact that I had no grievance against the lady, and that in any case the little trouble she might have given me would hardly have made me leave the Island that I loved so much.

As I have said, I left the Island convinced that I must return and even if possible live near by. That feeling remained with me all the time I was abroad. And then in early 1913, for no tangible reason whatever, I felt either that there was going to be a great movement in Ireland, or that it was necessary that some

8

movement should be launched that would require the active work of everybody that was willing to assist. This combined with that intense feeling I had about the Blaskets decided me to go back to West Kerry as near as possible to the island. They seem flimsy enough reasons to give for such a step, but they are the only reasons.

I had written from France to Willie Long at Ballyferriter to say that we were coming and asking him to look out for a house for us. Now I had arrived as far as Tralee. Romanticism and patriotic ardour both combined to present everything in an aspect of delight. The gloom of the grey March day, the moisture laden air, and the almost continual rain brought no depression, but brought back to mind similar days three years before when I had climbed to the highest points of the Island and walked along the ridge of the hills with the Atlantic occasionally appearing far beneath me through the mist. The fact that we should have to wait for hours before the little train was due to start for Dingle was not an inconvenience, but rather an assurance that here one escaped from the outer world of large towns and modern efficiency and haste.

I went into the post office to send a telegram saying that we had arrived so far. It would be late night before we reached Ballyferriter and the post office there would be closed. I wrote out my message, and as I went towards the counter a little old man stepped forward in front of me. His movements were still lithe, and he had eyes bright as a squirrel's.

'Is there any chance of getting tomorrow's pension today?' he asked of the girl behind the counter.

'There is not,' said she, and she looked across at me with a meaning nod of the head.

'Erra, why wouldn't 'oo give it to me?' said the old man in a wheedling tone.

'Is it to give it to you out of my own pocket and you may be to die on me before tomorrow and then where's I be.' The girl behind the counter rattled this out so rapidly that it was like one word. Indeed, it took me a couple of seconds to segregate

9

the words and grasp the meaning. But the many inflections of her voice indicated absolute finality. The old man accepted defeat. As he turned towards the door he looked across at me and said in a very 'resigned' tone, 'Them girls has no sense'.

I may have felt the tragedy of this old man who, now past seventy, looked to the Government to give him a pittance out of the public purse. But this was quite covered up by my delight in the dialogue and the voices, and the optimism of the old man who thought it natural that bureaucratic machinery should be adapted to suit his own convenience gave further assurance that I was drawing near to the end of my journey.

Even the wearisome delay of the train after its time to start pleased me. Officials moved excitedly about the platform beseeching the people to get in. Boys with bundles from shops were calling out names—'Mrs. O'Sullivan of Dingle', 'Mrs. Griffin, Aunascaul', and so on. An official would beseech a woman to get into the train. 'How can I go till the boy brings my parcels from Latchford's?' said she. 'Yerra, damn it ma'am, he's been bawling for you the last twenty minutes,' said the unfortunate official. But instead of insisting that the train must start, he went off to look for Latchford's boy in one direction while the woman went in another.

Somehow the train did go off at last. Besides ourselves there was one other man who was obviously not 'local', but I noticed that everyone seemed to know him, and that he spoke in Irish all the time. He got into conversation with me, to find out who I was and what I was doing there. I rather parried his questions, for I could give no straight answer. Certainly one of my reasons was that Irish was spoken in the West there and I wanted to acquire a good knowledge of the language, but that was hardly adequate. I also felt that a big national revival was due to take place, but I had no grounds for that. I also felt that I had to work to bring that national movement about, but if he had asked what I expected to happen or what I thought I should accomplish I should have looked foolish. Fortunately before such explanations were called for the train stopped suddenly. We all looked out to see what the cause was. It appeared that a donkey on the line had been struck by the engine. And my neighbour was called, to view the donkey. He looked at the beast, said it couldn't live, had it taken off the track and we all got back into the carriage and the train started off. No one took any further notice of the incident. My neighbour then explained that he was an official of the Department of Agriculture, and that was why he was called upon as an expert. Theoretically I objected to Government Officials. But he spoke Irish much better than I did, was enthusiastic for the language, and in politics an advanced nationalist. He knew every inch of that country and all the people. My enthusiasm was matched by his own. When we reached the end of the journey we were good friends.

Again on the platform at Dingle there seemed to be general excitement with people calling for parcels. I recognized a man from Ballyferriter and he brought me a note from Willy Long, explaining that he had not sent in his own jaunting car, as the night was so wild that he thought that we would prefer to stay in the hotel at Dingle for the night and go on to Ballyferriter the next day, but that if we decided to go straight on the bearer had a car and could bring us out. Of course we wanted to get on. The fact that the jaunting car was very old and inferior and the horse a poor one, meant nothing. And so we climbed up on the car, and piled on what luggage it would hold and started off in the black night.

It was a wild journey. The hail, instead of coming downwards from the sky was blown into our faces with the force of the strong wind. The footboard was so far below the seat that we could not touch it with our feet and consequently had no firm grip upon the car. Sometimes we could hear the sea roaring near at hand. Then we turned through the mountains. A wheel would go over a stone on the road and we would be nearly precipitated out into the dark. I had known that road fairly well, but in the utter blackness I could not see where we were. But at last I knew that we had crossed the peninsula for

11

I could hear the waves in Smerwick harbour. Away to the West there was now a sort of yellow light in the sky against which I could discern the outline of Sybil Head. Then we entered the road of the village with a light streaming out of Willy Long's door. The whole family came out to greet us. They showed us our rooms and had a meal ready. There again one's heart was uplifted. For Willy Long, living there in that remotest corner of Ireland, asked no more than to be able to serve his people without recognition. That was the reason for the welcome that he gave us. He might have been cynical about my coming there with my broken Irish, thinking that I was going to have some effect in preserving the language there where the people spoke it habitually. He might have been cynical about my coming there to preach self-sacrifice in the cause of Ireland to people who struggled to make a meagre living from a stony soil, and whose children must needs go off to America when they grew up, because there would be no means for them to make a living in their own place. But while Willy Long saw no merit in his own loving service of Ireland, he was always ready to appreciate anything done by another in the same cause.

In after years, when the Treaty was signed he sent me a note rejoicing in our success. And when the Civil War came and that part of the country was held by the Anti-Treaty party he was treated as an enemy of his country and persecuted. But when peace was restored and the power of the Free State Government established, and as a Minister my post consisted largely of letters demanding reward for services, or recompense for loss, or merely claims on the grounds of having met me, there was no letter from Willy Long. But after we went out of office, I was driving through Ballyferriter and called to see him. Again I received his welcome. He produced a meal. His house was mine. He stood in the background merely to see that we had all we required. He made no reference to any loss or suffering that he had endured, or to any service that he had given to his country—and how few had served her so devotedly and selflessly. His name appears in no list of heroes or patriots. His death was unrecorded.

In Willy Long's house old men used to gather at night. They would drink and talk. Naturally they talked in Irish. In fact they were mostly those who had the greatest interest in or knowledge of the language. They were like a literary circle, discussing old poems or stories or even words. One old man who had the nickname of 'Cais' or 'cheese' (no one could say why), was known as a poet. I never heard of any songs that he had made, but the more he drank the more difficult he was to understand. As everyone referred to him as a 'poet' I was anxious to follow all he said. But when I would turn to a neighbour to ask the meaning of a word that I did not know they usually admitted that it was also unknown to them. He was using words that were archaic—they were no longer in common usage amongst the people. What had happened was that these old men had grown up in an Ireland in which the language was in much more general usage. Most of them were probably born before the famine. Old 'Cais' in his youth had probably sat at the feet of other old men who went back to the eighteenth century, and had probably noted words that were already out of usage. Meanwhile as the area in which Irish was spoken shrank, and the number of Irish speakers diminished so also the language itself became impoverished. Words were only retained in so far as they were used in speech, for in a general way anything, and it was very little, that was published in Irish, did not reach those who naturally spoke the language. The result was that amongst Irish speakers there was a definite difference according to age. The old men had a wider vocabulary and used more complicated or idiomatic forms. An old man like 'Cais' in his youth was probably of what we should call 'the bookish type', but in his circumstances this was shown, not by acquiring books, which did not exist, and which he would not have been able to read, but by consorting with the old men of his time. But now the passage of time had operated. A young man in the district who was specially interested in Irish might come and sit with 'Cais' and store in his memory some of the things that 'Cais' had remembered in his own youth. But another young man with a certain feeling for literature would have comparatively easy access to newspapers, magazines and books in English. Thus there in that Irish-speaking district one could, as it were, watch the progressive death of the language. Not only was there a difference between the language of these old men from pre-famine days and that of the middle-aged men, but also between that of the middle-aged men and the younger generation. The old men spoke Irish all the time, even when they went into Dingle, the middle-aged spoke Irish at home in the village, but English when they went to town. And often even in Ballyferriter one would hear the younger men speaking English together.

That process has operated frequently in history. In ancient Gaul there must have been old men speaking Gaulish while their grandsons spoke Latin. And it may be that there were romantics among the young men who saw that a civilization, a lore, and a way of life would disappear with those old men, and dreamed of stemming the passage of time. I know that as I sat in that kitchen and listened to 'Cais' and his friends, or walked along the roads and was stopped by an old man who insisted on wandering off into old tales or quotations from old poems, I felt a sort of despair at the thought that as those old men died, so they took with them something that was recorded in no book and in no other mind.

This also gave one an exaggerated idea of one's own importance. The younger men thought of their lives before them. They had to make their living out of the land, or to go to America, and nothing that they could get from those long-winded ancients was likely to serve them for such purposes. It was all very well for officials of the Gaelic League to come around preaching about the language, or to listen to the old men with note books out. The young men would do the same thing if they were paid for it in the same way. There were

14

some indeed who did not agree that it was a great pity—that it was all a great pity. Some were language enthusiasts. But they were also going to get married, or had to run their farms. They could not live by merely listening to old men, who having reached the age for the old-age pension, had plenty of time to talk.

The other people whether in Dingle or on the countryside would respond to my sentimental romanticism very frankly.

'The Irishians come down here from Dublin' said one woman to me. 'They go out to the West and then come in here to Dingle, telling us about the wonderful girls out there, like princesses and speaking beautiful Irish. But I notice that none of them ever proposes marrying one of those wonderful western princesses.'

And when I spoke about one of these old men whose talk was like rich literature, the response was 'is it that old man, you mean. Yerra you could scrape the villainy off of him'.

The worst of it was that there was a certain amount of truth in what they said. At the beginning when I walked along the street in Dingle and an old man came along pouring out Irish at me, my heart went out to him, but I soon got to know that such an approach generally was a prelude to a suggestion that I should take him into a pub and stand him a drink, or give him a shilling. I must have found this rather trying for one day when the Irish College was in session in Dingle I was talking to two girls who were attending it, or rather to one of them who seemed to be a genuine enthusiast for the language. I knew that the other one wasn't, for one day she had turned to me with a puzzled look and said 'why the divil do you bother with this language when you aren't a teacher?' 'What has being a teacher got to do with it?' I said, 'And why do you bother with it?' 'Indeed it's far from this hole I'd keep, if I didn't have to get a certificate to keep my job,' said she.

While I was talking to them I saw an old man coming along who was easily distinguishable by the fact that part of his nose was lacking. 'I want to avoid that old fellow,' I said, 'he will

stop me to get a shilling for drink.' Then I felt the cynical
girl pressing her foot on mine while she frowned at me to say
no more. She afterwards explained that the old chap was the
other girl's uncle.

That was a happy time. I thought 'we are going to do something for Ireland', but I had no very clear idea of what it was
that we were going to do. Meanwhile the weather had cleared,
and on those bright days we went looking for a house. It might
be more correct to say that we went looking for places where
we should like a house to be. They were mostly the wildest
spots where there wasn't a house for miles. I remember climb-
ing over Marhin, and coming down the far side towards the
Cloach. Just where the Cloach crosses the ridge of the hills
seemed the most ideal spot imaginable. Underneath us to the
West the valley opened to the sea. We could see Dunquin
village and, beyond, the Blasket and its small brothers. The big
Blasket was like a big humped beast lying asleep on the surface
of the Atlantic. One could just see the houses in the island
village. And beneath us on the other side lay Ventry harbour
with Parkmore point stretching out like an arm sheltering it
from the rougher waters of Dingle Bay. On that sheltering arm
facing the harbour and on the edge of the water we saw a long
white house or building. There was a small dazzlingly white
strand just beside it, and then the long stretch of Ventry strand.
The most ideal spot for a house, we thought was the spot
where we were, at the top of the Cloach. But there was no
house there or anywhere near by. But that long white building
there on the side of the harbour with no other house near it,
with its little strand, and looking across the waters towards
Brandon Peak, and with its far side looking up Dingle Bay
towards Carran Tuohil and Mangerton that one saw in the far
distance, was only second to the perfect place. And of course
there was the very practical consideration, that the long white
house in that beautiful position was actually a house, whereas
the other place was only a spot on the side of a mountain.

We climbed back to Ballyferriter and enquired of the Longs

about the long white house, and the information they gave us justified hopes that we should be able to get it. It was Government property, and it was a matter of getting a lease from the Board of Works. A good Unionist relative hearing that our hearts were set on getting that house told us to leave it to him and he would arrange it all.

There was no reason to think that that would take long, but it was clear that when the lease was given the house would have to be put in order. We therefore decided to take a place temporarily. And for this purpose the only suitable place to be found was Ballintaggart, rather more than a mile to the east of Dingle.

Living so near to that little town I was naturally there frequently and got to know the people. They were all friendly, but the majority of them quite frankly failed to understand why anyone should want to live in the West when they had a choice of places. They could understand people coming for a holiday in the summer. Their own means of living was centred there and that explained their remaining. But I think that they must have regarded me as something of a lunatic. And though they were not lacking in patriotic feeling, the suggestion that I had chosen to go there to do something for Ireland probably added to their conviction that if I had no concealed object for going there I must indeed have some mental trouble.

Within two months of our arrival my intuitive conviction that we were on the eve of a national revival found something to feed upon. One morning, towards the end of April I called into a shop in Dingle and the owner said to me, 'why I was just talking about you. There is another man here on the same mission as yourself'.

I asked what she meant.

'He's not a minute gone,' she said. 'Indeed, he's worse than you are. He wants a job as a labourer with an Irish speaking farmer. He's ready to work without pay, so that he can stay here for two years.'

'Where is he,' I asked.

'He's looking for lodgings,' she said. 'I told him to try Mrs. O'Connor's. He's just gone off there now. You'll catch him on the way.'

I was already almost running after him. 'But what's his name?' I demanded.

'The funniest name you ever heard of, for a Gael', she said. 'Blight'. 'Here it is, he wrote it down for me.' She thrust a piece of paper across the counter to me. I glanced at it as I ran off. 'Ernest Blythe' was the name. But nobody in West Kerry ever pronounced it other than 'Blight'. Indeed they translated it into Irish as 'Blaisd', which means the blight that attacks potatoes.

I found him at Mrs. O'Connor's. He had just arranged to take lodgings with her for a few days. I immediately asked him to come home with me.

He had been as astounded at my presence as I was at his. 'What decided you to come and live here?' he asked.

I told him about my time on the Blaskets three years before, and the impression it had made upon me. And then the Census returns* showing the decay of the language, so that unless a change took place it meant that the last generation speaking Irish was the generation already alive. 'But I am convinced that there is a great national revival coming along,' I added. 'I can't say why I believe that, it is just a feeling in my bones.'

'That's just what I feel,' he replied. 'It is strange that we should both have that idea.'

He also had been affected by the Census returns. As a boy in the North, the girls that they employed on the farm had come from some place near Newry where Irish was spoken. He had been unable to understand why it was that he was Irish and yet could not speak the language. He had determined that when he grew up he must learn it. Then he had come to work in Dublin. There he immediately joined the Gaelic League, and learned some tiny smattering. In spite of the environment in which he had grown up as a Northern Protestant, he had been

* *Ed. note:* The Census of 1911.

nationalist from childhood, probably through his feeling that Irish language was the language that he should speak. As a result, when he came to Dublin, he had immediately sought out nationalist associations and become a disciple of Griffith. But after a few years in Dublin, and before he had really learned to make a good attempt at speaking the language, he had had to go back to a small provincial town in the North as a journalist on a local paper. There he could, if he liked, work with an Irish Grammar. But time was passing, and he found that where he was he was never likely to get any real grasp of the language, never likely to speak it and read it with any ease. The Census results had finally decided him. There was only one way to learn Irish, and that was to go and live where it was the natural language of the people. He had put by enough money to enable him to come and live in lodgings for about three months. That was far from being long enough for him to achieve what he had in mind, but he was going to cycle around and call on farmers to see if any would keep him in return for his labour on the land. And if he succeeded, he would stay for two years. At the end of that time he thought that he should have a command of the language that would put him in a position to work for the language thereafter. At the same time he wanted to work for a general national resurgence. But about that he was as vague as I was.

He fixed up about his lodgings and then came home with me, and we talked for the rest of the day. Nominally he came home with me in order that we might go over a map together, so that I should point out to him the areas where the people habitually spoke Irish, and give him the names of farmers that he might call on with his proposal to work for his keep.

That part of our business was soon settled, but we still talked and talked on into the night.

All the discouragement that I had experienced amounted to nothing when I found that the dreams that had germinated in my own mind had also germinated in Blythe's. That seemed a clear proof that we were both right. We both convinced each other, or rather convinced ourselves, that that dream was also germinating in thousands of other minds. That a sudden change was about to come over the country. That we were two swallows who made a summer.

After a few days spent on his bicycle riding all day round the country in pouring rain without success, Blythe got a letter from Dublin telling him to go to see people who lived on a small farm at Kinard east of Dingle but in a little spot where Irish was general. He went off there, and came back, as usual drenched to the skin, but with the news that he was now taken on as a labourer for his keep.

That meant of course that thereafter he was only with us for the week-ends. But we made the most of those week-ends. He arrived on the Saturday evening, and we talked far into the night. And on Sunday evening we still talked on, so that it was often two in the morning when I walked along the road with him on his way back towards the farmhouse where he worked.

We were both improving our Irish. He more than I, for he spoke nothing else from week-end to week-end. We also were becoming established as 'characters' in the district, and no doubt provided the people with subjects for their jokes. Also we made many friends. But we had certainly achieved nothing that was likely to alter the course of events.

We had practically no communication with the outside world of Nationalist Ireland, or with any organized body. But we felt that if we could win that little corner of West Kerry that the rest of the country would follow naturally.

Of course we talked of other things besides the language and the 'movement'. We were both interested in literature. I had a fairly big library of books. Blythe read them while he was with us at the week-ends, but he would never take back with him any book that was not written in Irish. He had imposed a sort of vow upon himself never to read or speak a word that was not Irish on his working days. But during the week-ends we would talk of literature and a hundred other matters. I knew quite a number of writers and painters in England and France and would tell stories of them. And Blythe would tell stories of well-known characters in Dublin and the North. We probably soon grew to think that we knew each other's friends intimately. I certainly regarded Sean O'Casey as a familiar figure. But I did not think of him as a dramatist or a writer. I knew rather about his enthusiasm for High Anglicanism, of the visits he had paid with Blythe to Church of Ireland dignitaries to get them to agree to have a service in Irish on St. Patrick's Day. And Blythe probably felt that he was intimately acquainted with T. E. Hulme and Ezra Pound, of whom I told him.

The summer was coming on. There were beautiful days when one could climb the mountains and look around on the unparalleled beauty of the country with sheer delight. And I must say that looking back on that time it is such days as those that come to my mind. But I do remember that we were looking forward to the coming of the O'Rahilly. He had a bungalow on Ventry Harbour where he and his family spent the summer. Neither of us knew him personally, but we knew about him. He was a regular contributor to Griffith's paper. We knew that West Kerry was the really important place, but at the same time Dublin had its significance. The people whose names we knew lived there. And when O'Rahilly came we should hear all that was stirring in the minds in Dublin.

Finally we heard that the O'Rahilly had moved in. I think he came to call on me. He was older than Blythe and I but he was not less of an enthusiast. He was enthusiastic about our action in going to live there. Nearly every time he came he greeted us with the words 'Ta plean agam' (I have a plan). Most of the plans were rather fantastic. Far from thinking us mad he must sometimes have thought we were painfully sane when we dealt with those plans.

We became fast friends immediately, and we were constantly together. Each of us treated the other's house as though it belonged to him. We discussed everything and laid down the law as to what was to be done. At the week-ends when

21

Blythe turned up we were able to lay before him all that we had decided in his absence.

Most people who came to West Kerry for holidays or to learn the language found their way to our house. Many of them I have lost sight of altogether since then, but even now I occasionally meet people that I have not seen since those days. There was a Protestant clergyman named Edward Thomas. But I do not think that he would like me to refer to him as a Protestant. He was ardently 'High Church' and intensely patriotic for Ireland. I have heard no more of him since 1919. Before he came to Dingle he had been for five years in Sicily. He was chaplain to the English people who are employed at Marsala. While there he had set about learning Irish. He had learned a great deal from books, but of course they could give him no idea of speaking the language. He attended the Dingle College of Irish and came out first in the written examination, though practically any of us could have made a better show at talking to a countryman on the road.

I think that he had taken the post in Sicily because there was no opening for him in Ireland. At that time advanced nationalism was a decided handicap to a Church of Ireland clergyman. And if besides that he suffered from the additional handicap of being High Church, there was little for him to do but to leave the country.

In 1918 when he was a curate in a village in Kerry, I heard that his political opinions were suspected by his parishioners, and that somebody inveigled him into giving expression to these opinions in a very frank way. Then there was a demand for his removal. I might think that was the last I heard of him, but that I remember that when a religious play of mine was produced at the Abbey Theatre in 1919, he wrote a review of it, and he was the only one who showed that he understood it. It remains in my memory because I was impressed by the irony of the fact that a play that set out to be specifically Catholic should, as far as one could judge, only be understood by a Protestant clergyman.

Among other visitors that I remember of that period were Robin Flower, who has continued visiting the Blaskets regularly since then, and Pierce McCann. I remember how everybody was charmed with Pierce. His good manners flowed naturally from his consideration for other people. The local people were impressed by the fact that he, a non-native speaker, spoke Irish well and at the same time had a knowledge of practical farming equal to their own. He was physically very strong, and could hold his own with any farmer in doing a day's work on the land.

I afterwards got to know him very well. For ten months we were interned together in Gloucester Gaol (1918–1919). In the end we were both removed to the same nursing home with influenza. I was much more ill than he when we were removed. But he died in the next room to me, as I was recovering.

With the summer came many other people also. But they were mostly only passers-by. There were people who came to the Summer College in Dingle, as a knowledge of Irish was necessary in their schools. There were also men, those who had jobs connected with the Gaelic League. A good many of them were more or less disciples of Griffith, but they did not go beyond that. Their presence was connected with their work, their earning of their daily bread, or with their play. But O'Rahilly was a man after our own heart. He was a full-time and unpaid worker. He was on holiday, certainly. We would swim together in the sea, drive about the country, climb mountains, and visit the people in their houses. We would sit up for hours talking about plans. Blythe and I were at times quite severely middle-aged in criticizing O'Rahilly's wildest plans. But, as a matter of fact, and in the light of the circumstances of that time, all our plans were wild. The Irish Party were in the Parliament at Westminster. Home Rule was in the air. The overwhelming majority of the people supported Redmond. In so far as that support had waned it was due to a growing cynicism among the people. Home Rule had been promised so

23

long and had not materialized. If it failed again there was no evidence to lead one to expect that the people would do more than shrug their shoulders and say that they expected as much.

On the other hand it did really look as though some Bill would actually become law. Those of us who thought of Home Rule as something utterly inadequate were a very small minority without influence, impotent. If we had been more critical of ourselves we should have been reduced to utter disheartenment. We dreamed of an armed uprising. But in the circumstances of the time, in the cold light of reason one could really have foreseen only the success of the Home Rule movement with a subordinate Government established whose restricted powers would be acclaimed as fulfilling all aspirations, or else the failure of Home Rule, which would have been accepted by the majority of the people as a proof that it was too much to hope for.

When O'Rahilly returned to Dublin at the end of the summer he was to take charge of the *Claidheamh Soluis*, the official organ of the language movement, which by definition was strictly non-political and non-sectarian. He had designed a new type, which while it should be Irish should be so modified that it could also be read by people who only knew the Roman script. It was to carry illustrations from photographs. It was to contain no English except one leading article a week, written by different people and signed. With O'Rahilly's energy behind it it was possible that the circulation of the paper might improve. But there was no real grounds for expecting any greater achievement than that. And the effect of that on the national position would certianly not be likely to change the course of national history. But if anybody had been present at the discussions we had about it, he might well have believed that it was the fulcrum required for moving the world.

CHAPTER THREE

The Volunteer Movement

The summer moved on to its end. The Irish College in Dingle closed, and there was a general exodus from the district. Strangers ceased to call. O'Rahilly was one of the last to leave, and when he and his family went one had a feeling of a certain desolation, that atmosphere of the holiday resort when the season is over. It had really been an exciting summer. But now we had to settle down to a quieter life. Fine weather alternated with storm. Old men would stop me on the road, and interlard their conversation with long quotations from Irish poems. I would call into cottages and the people would discuss other countries or cities that they had never seen, or they would tell stories, or we would discuss Irish politics. At the week-ends Blythe would come and we talked as usual, both conscious of O'Rahilly's absence. But we got news from Dublin. Without any reason whatever O'Rahilly felt the stirrings of new national impulses there. The new *Claidheamh Soluis* appeared under his control. It was brightened up with photographs of distinguished leaders of the language movement and similar people. The daily papers reflected a good deal of political excitement in connection with Home Rule. It seemed to be very near at hand. In the North a Volunteer movement had been formed to resist the application of the new law if it should become law. Then, when the new *Claidheamh Soluis* had been running a short time, Professor Eoin MacNeill wrote a leading article in English, headed with some such title as 'Why Not Irish Volunteers?' It was a suggestion that we also should form a volunteer movement, 'to maintain and defend the rights common to all the people of Ireland'. It was a sufficiently vague object, but its vagueness was intentional, designed to permit of the co-operation of all parties. It was conceivable that one who had hitherto been a Unionist asserting the right of the Parliament in Westminster to legislate for Ireland would participate in a movement that aimed at counteracting an attempt to prevent legislation by threatened force. The nationalist Home Ruler should find the proposal acceptable. If there was a danger that the British Government would abandon its programme before organized force in the North, then organized force in the South might encourage it to go ahead and fulfil its promise.

As for the more 'advanced' nationalists such as we were, they had long dreamed of an armed military movement. The I.R.B. advocated that as its cardinal doctrine. As a matter of fact it had already decided to take some steps to that end.

At the same time it is more than likely that most of those (and they could not have been very many) who read the article, probably thought of it as an interesting idea, not intended to be more than a topic of discussion. O'Rahilly wrote to call my particular attention to this article, though he need not have done so. I pointed it out to Blythe though he had probably already seen it.

At this stage I should mention that before Blythe came to Kerry he had been empowered by the Irish Republican Brotherhood to receive suitable recruits for that organization. I had become a member, and we were in touch with headquarters in Dublin in the person of Mr. Bulmer Hobson.* O'Rahilly did not belong to the I.R.B. at that stage, and when he wrote to say that Professor MacNeill had been into the office to ask could

* *Ed. note:* Ernest Blythe dates Desmond FitzGerald's enrolment in the I.R.B. later. See footnote on pp. 50–51.

26

not something be done to give practical effect to the proposals contained in his article, Blythe urged me to write to O'Rahilly pressing him to go ahead. This I did, but again this was quite unnecessary. For in the office of the *Claidheamh Soluis* there was a young man, a member of the I.R.B., who promptly reported MacNeill's suggestion to his superiors in the organization and he was instructed to give an assurance that if a public meeting was called for the purpose of founding a volunteer organization a minimum of five hundred could be guaranteed to be present. It was therefore announced that a meeting for the purpose of promoting an Irish Volunteer Movement would be held in the Rotunda on November 13th. Blythe and I were jubilant down in Kerry. We anxiously awaited news of the meeting. Then came the newspapers supplemented by letters from O'Rahilly and other friends. Not only was the Hall filled, but overflow meetings had to be held. The number present was given as seven thousand. That was probably an exaggeration, but it was clear that the attendance had been such that if the guaranteed five hundred had not turned up, they would hardly have been missed.

Of course, the large numbers present and the great success of the meeting, did not in any way indicate that the people agreed with us. The truth was that the moment was well chosen. The existence of the so-called Ulster Volunteers had been made the supreme argument against Home Rule in English political circles. The ordinary Irish Nationalist was indignant that after a constitutional struggle lasting for more than a generation it should be defeated in the end by a mere threat of forceful resistance.

But the meeting had been promoted by no political organization. It flowed from the article in the *Claidheamh Soluis*, the official organ of the Gaelic League, and the League was defined as non-political. Its prime mover had been Eoin MacNeill, known to be a nationalist, and a pioneer in the Gaelic movement, but with no political party label. With him there were associated men who were well-known supporters of the Irish

27

Party, and others well known as advocating a more 'advanced' national policy. But the Irish Party officially had remained aloof. They certainly did not anticipate any outcome from the meeting. They had probably never dreamed that the British Government would cower before the threat of force from the North, and the Tory Party backers of the North.

Blythe and I, getting the news and reviewing it in a completely partisan spirit, saw it as a great victory. Here was a movement launched on military or quasi-military lines independent of the official Parliamentary Party but received enthusiastically by the people, with columns of the ordinary daily papers devoted to it. As the Irish Party were not in charge of it, it meant that our friends would be so, inevitably. The fact that our friends had promoted it, and that for them it was the all important movement, while the supporters of the Irish Party who had associated themselves with it regarded it as at best an auxiliary that might possibly be of use, and at worst might be a nuisance, meant that the enthusiasm of our friends would necessarily make their influence preponderate. Also the very nature of the movement meant that it must tend towards our political form.

A Volunteer Executive was formed on which our side easily preponderated. MacNeill was President, O'Rahilly one of the Treasurers. Branches were formed in Dublin, and halls were taken where men were drilled. I don't suppose that many of the men who drilled expected ever to be called upon to take up arms and fight. I think they and the public generally regarded it more as a gesture to counteract the similar (and opposite) gesture in the North. We should have liked them all to be consciously preparing to fight for Irish freedom, but we did not delude ourselves that that could be said of more than a minority.

In West Kerry the people seemed to be interested in the Volunteers as an item of news in the papers rather than as an organization that they might join in themselves. In any case neither Blythe nor I was able to get any companies started before Christmas.

We were due to go to Belfast for Christmas. We went up to Dublin taking our Blasket Island maid with us. I stayed with O'Rahilly passing to and from Belfast. I had been seeing the newspapers and receiving letters from him and other friends. Blythe and I had discussed what these contained with enthusiasm, but I looked forward to being on the spot, and to hearing directly from those who were controlling the movement how it was going and what the prospects were. Of course I found O'Rahilly full of enthusiasm. Several nights during the week he was attending halls and drilling men, or supervising their drill. He was attending meetings of the Executive, and had great hopes of spreading the movement over the country and making it the most active and largest national organization. Naturally he and I were both full of the new movement. With him I attended various drills and meetings, and went to see some of the leaders. Most of them impressed me as being unduly pre-occupied with Dublin. Nevertheless they all urged that we should push the movement ahead in Kerry. It was then that I first met Professor MacNeill and Cathal Brugha. I had a number of talks with Bulmer Hobson. I probably went to him in the first place with Blythe. For in Kerry Blythe constantly referred to him with much deference, and I accepted Blythe's estimate of people known to him and unknown to me. Hobson assured us that all was going well and that the movement would be clearly directed towards a rising. O'Rahilly also presumed an armed revolt, but he was not a member of the I.R.B. while Hobson was in its inner councils, so we took his word as more authoritative.

Naturally enough I went to see Mr. Griffith. I had met him before but had had very little opportunity of talking to him. But now we became good friends. Indeed looking back now it seems that that strong affection that bound us together in after years began during those few days in Dublin. It was not strange that I should have felt affection for him. I had followed him since my early teens. And now getting to know him I realized that one could admire him not merely because of the clarity of

29

his thought, but also for the beauty of his character, his utter selflessness in his devotion to Ireland, and his extraordinary modesty. I was a very young man of no importance, but that did not matter to him. It was as though he felt a deep personal gratitude to anyone who made even a little attempt to help his cause. Another thing that impressed me about him was his understanding of Ireland in her totality. One night I went to a meeting in No. 6 Harcourt Street where somebody read a paper and afterwards Alderman Tom Kelly made a speech that was probably quite amusing, but it revealed to one a mentality incapable of conceiving an Ireland that was other than Dublin and its immediate surroundings. The Ireland that I knew was far away in the South-West where the people only occasionally spoke English. The Alderman's speech indicated that that Ireland had no existence for him. In West Kerry there still survived a life that went back unbrokenly to a remote Irish past. Whereas for the Dublin Alderman the past only brought to mind the glories of the eighteenth century capital that was second only to London, that was akin to London, and hostilely alien to the mere Irishry in the remainder of the country. I remember thinking that it was impossible for people living in Dublin to have anything in common with the people of the South-West. But I spent the later part of the evening with Griffith, and found that though he belonged to Dublin and knew every corner of it, by some intuitive power he was able to transcend his environment and to understand all Ireland, and to love her not as an abstraction or as a locality, but as a living reality.

Going on to Belfast I moved into a completely Unionist milieu.* But while Blythe was there we arranged to meet occasionally. On one occasion the two of us together with Sean Lester went to a meeting of some youthful 'Republican' association. Sean Lester had been converted by Blythe from Unionism to a nationalism of our own colour. One felt sorry for him living in Belfast.

We three appeared to be very adult at the meeting. But the

* *Ed. note:* Staying with his wife's family.

youthful members showed an extraordinary grasp of all the formalities of a public meeting, rising on points of order and moving amendments. Two of James Connolly's daughters made most impressive speeches. But when the business of the meeting was concluded the suppressed youthfulness of the members asserted itself largely in the form of horse-play. I got a kick on the ankle from two youthful republicans who were rolling on the floor.

Blythe went back to Kerry while I was still in Belfast. He had to get back to his work as a farm labourer. After he left I only had one escape from unadulterated Unionism, and that was one night when we went round to Joseph Francis Biggar's. I spent most of the evening with Sir Roger Casement. I never saw him again after that. We discussed every aspect of the movement and our national aspirations. But while I was young and enthusiastic and unconscious of what was involved, he could more correctly be described as grave and earnest. He comes before the eye of the mind as he stood there that evening in a tweed suit, while we whispered together about the armed Rising that must take place. I can realize now that while we talked he realized the enormous gravity of what we planned. It is not hard to convince myself that he was conscious that those plans involved his own execution.

When I came back to Kerry after Christmas I brought with me a commission to organize Volunteers there in the West. I gave Blythe a detailed account of all I had seen and heard in Dublin. Then I went into Dingle to call on various people to propose to them that we should start volunteers there. I was astounded to find how ready they were. Indeed it seemed that they had already been discussing it. A meeting was called for some night*
and it was attended not only by a large number, but also by the

* *Ed. note:* Ernest Blythe points out that the author's memory has telescoped events at this stage. The inaugural meetings did not take place until 18th and 19th April, a week after the presentation of the plays described on p. 34. This is confirmed by the Kerryman of 25th April 1914.

'influential' people of the town, men who certainly did not share the political views of Blythe and me. But they urged the people to support the movement, and allowed their names to go forward as members of the Committee who were to take charge. This was important, particularly from the financial side. It meant that they would subscribe to our fund and that the people generally would follow their example. They would not, of course, take part in parades or drills, but that also was to the good.

When we had first met in the previous April we had talked about things that were going to happen, but we had not had any tangible notion of what we meant. Now it seemed that things were happening. We probably thought of ourselves as having had prophetic instincts. But if at this stage we had stopped to think over the matter we should have seen that all that had happened was that we and others in other parts of the country were drilling men, and exhorting them to patriotism, but that the drilling had no immediate objective. It was taken to be a gesture in support of Home Rule, showing that we were just as determined to secure and maintain our rights as others were to deny them to us. Among the men who were being drilled by us and by others there were some who agreed with us that ultimately Irish freedom would be won by unconstitutional methods. Others were coming to accept that view. But there was still much more of the boyish dream in our talk about the coming fight than there was of an event fixed for a certain date. It had long been taken for granted in our circles that a war was inevitable, and that that war would be between England and Germany. And we talked of a rising in arms when that war should take place. But we presumed more than the war. We took it for granted that in such a war the Irish people would necessarily be sympathetic with the side opposed to England, and we presumed also that that side would probably be victorious. We did not know how near or how far off that war might be, and I cannot now remember how we expected it to develop. We may have thought of England being blockaded, and invaded. But probably we were content not to go into such details. A war would come in which, at last, England would be the vanquished. Our very vagueness on this point meant that it lacked much conviction. I suppose that we were, to some extent, romanticists. For more than a generation our country had sent representatives to the British Parliament, to plead for the establishment of a subordinate Irish Parliament, while the people were growing more and more sceptical as to the attainment even of that. We were subconsciously aware that the continued decay of the Irish language was bringing ominously near a further great break with our past. On the one hand it seemed that an intensification of ardent nationalism would revive the language—that it could not otherwise be revived; and on the other hand we probably felt that that resurgence of intense nationalism, would itself unite us to that almost dead past. Irishmen volunteering to train for the defence of their rights would gradually become conscious that they possessed national rights, rights that had their roots in our racial past.

The talk of the approaching war contained an element of realism, as it was a recognition that a new element, a new condition was necessary to give hope to any attempt to put Irish physical force against British power. But that is about the extent of the realism. It would be ridiculous to point to the fact that the war did actually happen as a proof of our wise sizing up of the situation. It would be like the case of a man who having picked a horse blindfolded with a pin, thereafter posed as an expert judge of horseflesh.

To have men arming for the declared purpose of serving Ireland was an achievement, even if the men did not anticipate that they would ever make use of their arms. And I think that the party spirit was not entirely absent from our minds. On the whole we rather hoped and expected that the Home Rule Bill would become law, but we looked upon the Irish Party as enemies. They treated all who disagreed with them, all who thought their method lacking in national dignity, as cranks and soreheads. But now the Volunteer movement was the main

33

Irish political activity. It was independent of control by the Irish Party, and it was very evident that the leaders of the party were gravely concerned by this fact.

The Irish language fell rather into the background, although Blythe organized a company of actors in his district for the production of some short plays in Irish. The rehearsals were quite popular as they provided social gatherings for the young people. When all was ready he offered to produce the plays for a charity in Dingle provided the potential beneficiaries would cover all expenses. The only hall big enough to hold those who bought tickets was L-shaped. The result was that rather more than half of those who attended had no chance whatever of seeing the stage. And as they had come for an evening's entertainment they were determined to have it. They sang and shouted and were generally uproarious, enjoying themselves thoroughly. The result was that those who had bought the more expensive tickets which entitled them to seats in that part of the hall which gave a view of the stage were unable to hear a word of the dialogue. They, therefore, joined in the hilarious uproar. The actors themselves were affected by the general gaiety and rose to the occasion splendidly. At the end when actors and audience surged out into the dark streets they were still exhilarated and exultant about the grand evening's entertainment they had had. Blythe was far too philosophical to feel aggrieved that this was all that came of his labour in training the Company.*

If we had been ready to accept discouragement we might have found plenty of grounds for it. When we made speeches about a new free Ireland with her own army, and with international recognition, somebody else would make a speech in support of us in which the Home Rule Bill was spoken of as fulfilling all our national aspirations. And even more discouraging still might have been the fact that as the applause of our noble sentiments died away, some 'character' would get up to the great delight of the audience and make a speech of

* *Ed. note:* The plays were presented on 12th April 1914.

34

grotesque buffoonery which, of course, was the popular event of the evening and received much wilder applause than we could hope for. I was largely responsible for this, for I insisted that the rule of the Volunteers that the movement was open to every Irishman should be most rigidly applied and refused to exclude a man merely because he belonged to the tramp class or was a well-known bad character, or was partly imbecile, and these characters always sought an opportunity to make themselves prominent, and considered that they deserved a reward for doing so. It frequently happened that a man who had turned everything to ridicule would propose to me that I should stand him a few drinks after the event. Their endeavours were probably rewarded, but not through Blythe or me. We were both rigidly puritanical. We took it for granted that the service of Ireland imposed an asceticism upon all. In fact, just before the Volunteer movement had been launched, Blythe had elaborated a scheme for a sort of monastic institution to which men should dedicate themselves for the purpose of promoting the Irish language. They were to undertake that they would not get married for five years (it was to be a celibate organization) and they were not to drink. I forget if smoking was to be allowed. They were to support themselves by their own communal labours, and devote the remainder of their time to teaching the language and working on its behalf.

We were all the time calculating our gains, and on this side we found many grounds for congratulation. In that simple community of people struggling to earn their daily bread there was a deep-seated love of Ireland that demanded no party label. Middle-aged men, and elderly men whose memories went back far into the nineteenth century had supported the various national movements from Fenianism to Parnell and Redmond. The long deferred promises had not disheartened them. They were ready to answer to any call even including the call for financial assistance out of their small means.

When it was proposed that there must be a collection for the Volunteers I was far from optimistic. It was taken for granted

35

that I was to head the party of collectors, and it was a work that I should gladly have avoided if I could have made a good case for so doing. Before the collection began, the committee began calculating how much the collection would yield. This seemed to me ridiculous until we got on to the work. Then I found that no one thought of demurring. It was a national cause that involved no party differences. The people merely asked how much they were to give. It was apparently a long established custom that in such cases people gave according to their valuation. When we went round the poorer houses out in the West, I was often ashamed to take the money when I looked round and saw the stark conditions under which the people lived. And yet as often as not it was clear that if we had asked them to increase their contributions they would have given without demur.

This money was required for ordinary expenses including the payment of drill instructors, but also for the purchase of arms. I know that we were among the first to send money to Dublin for this latter object. But the arms did not arrive until long afterwards.

We were notified that a parade of Volunteers from all parts of Kerry would be held in Tralee, where they would be reviewed by a Mr. Talbot-Crosbie.* Of course our companies must be present. We felt that ours were the most imbued with the true doctrine. I therefore spent the evening of the last drill before the parade urging upon the men the importance of bringing credit upon the company at the parade on Sunday. Particularly I stressed the importance of avoiding drunkenness. For going to Tralee meant catching the morning train and waiting for the train back which left only in the evening, hours after the parade would be over. And there would be nowhere to spend that time but in public houses.

After we arrived in Tralee I was told that the leaders of all

---

* *Ed. note:* In the original typescript this description of the Talbot-Crosbie meeting appeared on p. 53, but it has been transposed in order to place it in its proper context chronologically.

Volunteer companies were to call at a certain place to see a priest who was associated with the movement. I went and discovered that this was because there were rumours of a split in the Volunteers and we were urged to do nothing and to say nothing that would imply a lack of unity. I did not receive this too graciously. Nevertheless I accepted the instruction assuming that it was merely a matter of avoiding anything upon which there might be different opinions, and I certainly assumed that the Mr. Talbot-Crosbie would have the same instructions.

The various companies were paraded in a large field that was a market. The man who was to review them mounted upon the roof of a shed, from which he could see and address all those present. He referred too to rumours of dissension in our ranks, and scoffed at them. And to show that we were all at one he called for three cheers for Mr. Redmond, which was responded to by most, but not by Blythe or by me. We were infuriated. The whole meeting had been given the appearance of a demonstration that we all supported the policy of the Irish Party. We could do nothing but remain silent. Then all the Volunteers were taken marching round the town. It was dry weather and therefore we were not splashed with the peculiarly fine sticky mud that one generally associated with those streets. But the peculiar quality of that mud was due to the fact that the stone of the district made a very fine powder, and now we walked through a cloud of dust, which made our faces and our clothes a dirty white. Muddy perspiration ran down our faces. Our throats were parched, and still the march continued. It did not end until we were exhausted, and when it was over we had nothing to do but to hang about that town for hours until the Dingle train would start. From our point of view it was a disastrous day. It was just as well that I did not meet the priest who gave us our instructions, for it would have been a rancorous interview.

At the next drill in Dingle I found that the men seemed to have gone backwards. I tackled one man who seemed incapable

of forming fours and asked him what was the matter. He replied,
'Erra, the way it is, after all you said about keeping away from
drink, I drank so much lemonade last Sunday in Tralee that I
haven't been the same man since. I can do nothing with my
feet'.

His experience was so like my own that I could not find any
more fault with him.

Those of us who belonged to the 'advanced' section talked
among ourselves (and we were adding to our numbers) about
the armed conflict that was to take place when England would
be in difficulty, though we could not name any approximate
date when that would occur. The interest of the others was
kept alive by the news in the daily papers. And, indeed that
news was just as interesting for us. The development of the
movement was a major item of news. Every day there were
reports of big meetings and parades, of new branches formed,
of addresses by Volunteer leaders. New elements, such as the
Curragh Mutiny in March 1914, entered into the Home Rule
situation. The whole position of Home Rule was jeopardized
by truculence and threats from the North, and British Officers
refused to accept their orders from their Government against
whom the truculence and threats were directed. If a mere
'contingent belligerency' in the North was so effective that the
British Government would allow a mutiny in their Army to go
unpunished, and waver about the fulfilment of a decision of
Parliament, then the appropriate line of action for us was a
more than 'contingent belligerency' in the rest of Ireland. The
Irish people were demanding merely that a promise should
be fulfilled, and that the decision of Parliament should be law.
If the threat from the North created a new situation that justified a reversal of a parliamentary decision, then a threat from
the South might appropriately justify a reversal back again.
And there was also this difference. The Ulster Volunteers had
been promoted by politicians to be a weapon, an argument, in
their political moves. It was more than doubtful if they had any
intention of turning that threat into a reality. Our movement
38

was to a large extent controlled and permeated with those who had already determined that the Volunteers should ultimately move from the position of threat to that of action. If the British Government were really afraid of a rebellion in Ireland, they could be put into the position of having to choose between possible rebellion in the North and actual rebellion in the remainder of the country.

But when I have said that, I have to modify it. Even among ourselves we had constantly to posit a new condition, that of war between England and a European Power equal to herself, as a condition precedent to an open Rising. And at that time, that required condition was only a possibility. The public in general certainly did not anticipate that the military form of the new movement was directed to military action. They regarded it rather as a political argument, 'equal and opposite' to the political argument of the Ulster Volunteers. The man in the street, if he thought of the situation that would result from the abandonment of Home Rule by the British Government, certainly did not assume that the Volunteers would take to the field.

I cannot undertake to tell what was in other people's minds, but from conversations that I had from time to time with men on our side who were more or less prominent in the movement, it seemed that their minds worked on these lines.

It is undignified for a nation to confine itself to purely constitutional action in the Parliament of their overlords. In such a condition the most that they can demand is that a subordinate legislature shall be created. The decision to grant or to withhold that demand is governed largely by considerations of political party advantage in the governing country, or at best in relation to the interior political conditions of that country. But when a military or quasi-military organization asserts a national demand, the claim it formulates is no longer limited, indeed it can only tolerate the minimum limitations upon complete autonomy, and it offers a new inducement for the satisfaction of its demands, for it is a source of internal weakness to the governing power, and in the event of a war, or the threat of a war whose outcome is uncertain, it may well be worth the while of the governing power to go to the farthest limits to remove that weakness. It gains nothing by continuing to assert its domination, it may gain much by relinquishing its grip.

But the truth is that such discussions as brought out these views were generally regarded as more or less irrelevant, merely interesting speculations. What really mattered was that the new type of movement would necessarily create a new, more exigent, and more virile national spirit in the country. The British Government, by its own pusillanimity over the Northern Unionists and English Tories must stand idly by while the movement extended itself through the country. And the Irish Party could no longer put forward the old argument that any suggestion of a departure from constitutional methods would injure the national cause by alienating English opinion, for it had been demonstrated that unconstitutional action had a much greater effect upon English opinion than parliamentary argument.

But to get back to my narrative, in April 1913, Blythe and I had confided to each other that we felt that we were on the eve of a period of more intense nationalism in Ireland. We had not been able to point to any premonitory symptoms of such a revival, but by April 1914 we considered that the feeling in our bones had already proved to be prophetic.

That year O'Rahilly was not able to take his usual long holiday down there in the West. To the best of my memory as a member of the Executive and joint treasurer, he was kept in Dublin, and had to go to various parts of the country to address meetings and hold reviews.*

* *Ed. note:* Ernest Blythe recalls at least one visit by O'Rahilly in the Summer of 1914 and this is confirmed by the Kerryman which on 8th August 1914 reported that O'Rahilly had 'arrived in Dingle for his customary annual holiday'. Ernest Blythe remembers him staying for only two nights, however, adding:

There were also other matters to keep him away from the West. From the very foundation of the Volunteers the matter of arms had been the most important point to our minds. A certain amount of armament was being obtained. In April the Northern Volunteers landed a cargo of rifles, and I think that it must have been some time after that that O'Rahilly informed me that we also were going to run guns. He had proposed that the vessel running them should unload them in batches at various lonely parts of the coast, one of which was to be at my house. But that proposal was either not accepted or was abandoned as it is well known that it was ultimately decided to land them on the east coast at Howth and Kilcoole, an event which actually took place towards the end of July.

But even before that date everything seemed to combine to strengthen the Volunteer position. The period of the House of Lords veto expired and Home Rule should have been law in June, but before that date the British Government began proposing further concessions to be made to those who were opposed to Home Rule. The date of the application of the new law was postponed, and it was clear that if it ever came into effect the powers it would confer on the new Irish Parliament would be curtailed, or the area of jurisdiction of that parliament would be diminished. This seemed to prove the case that we

'He came for two days just before Britain declared War. His visit was to get me, as a man with no job and no dependants or strong family ties, to go to Germany to represent the Irish Volunteers. When word came to Kinard that he wanted to see me, I went to Cuan (Desmond FitzGerald's home on the south shore of Ventry Bay) that night, and next morning Desmond and I walked around to the bungalow (O'Rahilly's bungalow on the north side of the bay). O'Rahilly took me into another room while Desmond remained talking to Madam O'Rahilly. I declined to go to Germany because I knew that the I.R.B. was sending someone, probably Casement. Anyhow I could not go without I.R.B. permission. I did not, however, mention the I.R.B. to O'Rahilly whom I knew not to be a member. He went back to Dublin next day very angry with me. Before he spoke, O'Rahilly pledged me to secrecy. So I may not have given Desmond any hint of what his business was. Therefore, there would be nothing to fix in Desmond's memory that O'Rahilly in 1914 came to Ventry for two nights.'

41

had been making all along. The result of forty years of constitutional action was cancelled by the mere fact that men in the North had armed. That was clearly a more effective argument with the British Government. We could use that argument much more pointedly. The leaders of the Volunteers were assuming a greater importance in the eyes of the people than the parliamentary leaders.

At this point* Redmond demanded that his nominees should be accepted upon the Executive of the new organization. We, in Kerry, took it for granted that our own friends on the Executive, those who shared our views, would stand out against this. But they assented to it. I wrote a furious letter to O'Rahilly, but when I saw him, he explained that he and others had assented, as the all important thing was to maintain the organization and to go ahead with arming the men. If Redmond's demand were refused there was every prospect that the Volunteer organization would be killed or at least split in such a way that only our own immediate supporters would remain with it. Whereas the mere fact of bearing arms would automatically turn men's minds to a greater measure of freedom than Home Rule offered.

During that summer also, the war that we had spoken of and prophesied, more from a desire to justify our belief in an armed rising than from any perspicacious reading of the time, seemed to be moving towards a reality.

I notice that now pacifists usually talk of war as the product of the callous cynicism of age and middle age and of youth as standing for peace. But my own experience does not bear that out. I can recall conversations with Blythe and with other friends, none of us past our middle twenties. We spoke with a lofty superiority of Daniel O'Connell, because we understood that having seen something of the French Revolution in his youth, all during his later life he had been determined to avoid the ways of war. And we spoke of John Dillon in the same way

* *Ed. note:* Mid June 1914.

because we had heard that he had said that after what he saw of the sufferings endured by the people in the extra-constitutional activities of the nineteenth century, he would never sanction a return to such methods. But to our unimaginative youth it seemed unworthy of Irish freedom that it should be won other than by the sword. And that required, if it were to have any hope of success, that there should be a major conflict between Britain and some other power. We should have thought it most natural that we should take any action that might produce that condition. But there was nothing we could do. The world was quite unaware of our existence. We were drilling country boys and village boys at the end of a most westerly peninsula, and we were making speeches to country people in whom a very noble traditional patriotism had in no way diminished a highly developed sense of humour and of the ridiculous.

A woman serving me across the counter in a shop would say quite simply:

'Yerra, we all know that you and Mr. Blight are quite mad, but ye mean well according to ye're lights.'

Ireland was hardly known in Europe, the leaders we followed were hardly known to the people of Ireland, and we were only in charge of the movement in one remote part of the country. But everything seemed to happen as it would have done if it were responding to our wills. The men of Ireland were arming for the purpose (at least nominally) of maintaining and defending the rights common to all the people of Ireland. We had no doubt that when it came to defining what exactly that meant, it would be stated as something very like our own doctrine. And the condition of war that was required to offer any conceivable prospect of success to the method of armed rising seemed a real possibility.

But, writing it that way, may easily give the impression that our minds and our plans were much more clear cut than they actually were. It suggests that we conceived of the Volunteers as a force drilling and arming with a view to a predetermined rising of which only the date was vague. But that was hardly

43

the case. There may have been one or two who had their minds made up that a Rising there must be. But, as far as I can judge from various conversations that I had at that time with some who later were to take the lead in promoting the Rising, they rather regarded such action as a possible outcome. What we wanted immediately was a more intensive nationalism, that would have aspirations that would be far from met by the mere grant of a subordinate parliament. Representation in Westminster was an implicit recognition of the British Government as the Government of Ireland.

The acceptance of the doctrine of physical force was a repudiation of that British claim. The fact that men were drilling and arming in the service of Ireland had its own logic that would force them to assert Ireland's claim, would cause them to reject all those who minimized that claim, and would direct them into a path of more ardent national service in all spheres.

We had talked of a coming war which should be England's difficulty and our opportunity, but the people must be ready to avail themselves of that opportunity to assert the maximum claim, and prepared to fight if that claim were not granted. But that moment of difficulty was to be brought about by others not by us. And it was possibly a sort of dogma with us that that difficulty would be so acute that England would yield to our demands to avoid a worse evil.

The thought of Ireland rising in arms was certainly a glorious dream. Irrespective of a future war and whether it would create a situation that would make it possible for us to overcome the British power in Ireland by force, we were still convinced that an armed movement was the most effective way of producing a spirit in the country that would assert the true claim when the moment came, and that when that moment came, this armed movement would be the greatest argument in Ireland's hands to get that claim accepted. That had been our belief all along. The sight of England cowering before the threat of the Orangemen, and the spectacle of the British Government trying to buy off armed opposition in the North at the expense of Ire-

44

land's claims, was merely a visible proof of what we had all along maintained.

If we had been older and wiser we should probably have regretted that the declaration of war came when it did, that it had not remained as a danger threatening, but, as a matter of fact, when war came our immediate reaction was that it was a cause for rejoicing. That was quickly followed by disappointment.

We could remember that in our childhood, the whole of Irish sympathy had gone out to the Boers. And we knew that in the various little wars of the nineteenth century, Ireland had always been on the side of England's enemies. That attitude could have been amply justified by the fact that on all these occasions those fighting against England had been weak peoples defending their own countries. But the fact that the Irish people had regarded England as their own enemy, holding their country by force would in any case have decided to which side their sympathy should go. Of course, in every war there had been many Irishmen fighting on England's side, but we disregarded that. We looked upon them as men who had yielded to the pressure of economic circumstances. The mass of the people had given their sympathy to the side opposed to England.

The truth is that in spite of our hectic drilling, and our constant insistence that the national movement must be armed, we were more intent upon the doctrine than its application in force. We had talked of an armed Rising, but to a large extent it had been from 'the lips out'. We had not really set out to visualize it internally. It had been something remote, contingent upon circumstances that we could not control, and therefore far-off.

As the signs accumulated that the conflict in Europe would indeed become an actuality we had a sensation of catching our breath. This was what we had spoken of for so long. But we had spoken of it as a war in which England would be beaten at last. Then came the news that war was declared between England and Germany. Looking back at that time now, I can

45

see that according to what we had been preaching we should have been disappointed that it had come so soon. But youth is irresponsible and impatient. I think that our first reaction was one of jubilation. England would now be beaten, and a resurgent Irish Nationalism would assert and make effective our claim to real autonomy.

Even now we did not fully visualize a Rising. We probably thought of Germans landing in England and in Ireland, of our making an alliance with them, and, when the war ended in England's defeat, and the Germans evacuated these islands, an Irish Government would take control in Ireland, while England would settle down to the position of a minor power.

Any exultation we felt was probably mingled with a breathlessness at the consciousness that our movement would now have to shoulder a huge responsibility. At the back of our minds was an awareness that a mere condition of war did not attain our promised land for us.

And whatever degree of exultation possessed us soon gave way to a condition very close to despair. On the very declaration of war, Mr. Redmond made a statement assuring the English people that the Irish Volunteers would protect Ireland. On the face of it that statement could be interpreted as perfectly legitimate. The purpose of the Volunteers was to maintain and defend the rights common to all the people of Ireland, but no vestige of those rights had yet been attained. Our country was still held by England, and the statement in the House of Commons clearly meant that the Volunteers would defend that English possession called Ireland against Germany.

But more disturbing than that mere statement was the fact that it immediately became apparent that it really represented the views of the majority of the Irish people. It was galling enough to have England's control brought home to us by the placards in post offices and outside police barracks calling on Irishmen to 'Join the British Army', but the daily papers that reached us the day after they were published assumed that it was most natural that we should flock to join that Army at this moment of England's danger. It was assumed also that the declaration of war by the British Government automatically made Germany the enemy against whom the meagre arms of the Volunteers were to be directed. And it appeared from those newspapers that that doctrine was accepted by the Volunteers themselves. There were reports of the success of recruiting and of Volunteer bands marching to the station to see off their comrades who had volunteered for service in the British Army. The movement on which all our dreams had centred seemed merely to have canalized the martial spirit of the Irish people for the defence of England. Our dream castles toppled about us with a crash. If Irishmen had served England in previous wars in their thousands it was clear that in this war they would serve her in their tens of thousands. It was brought home to us that the very fever that had possessed us was due to a subconscious awareness that the final end of the Irish nation was at hand. For centuries England had held Ireland materially. But now it seemed that she held her in a new and utterly complete way. Our national identity was obliterated not only politically but also in our own minds. The Irish people recognized themselves as a part of England.

Of course I wrote to O'Rahilly in Dublin to ask him how could he, and the other members of the Executive who felt as he did, and to whom we looked to give the country a lead, fail to break with Redmond and continue to sit with the Redmond nominees on the Executive. The reply came back telling me not to worry, that all was well, that our friends had not been swept off their feet by the general landslide.

But there was little comfort in that letter. Blythe and I had chosen to live there in the remote West because we thought that there where the language and a more traditional way of life still subsisted was the most truly Irish part of our country. This now seemed to be more true than ever. The news that came from the outer world all conspired to show the rest of the country as spiritually and nationally absorbed by England. The Irish nation had shrunk to a small corner in the West.

47

Once we had got to that point of despair, we might as well have gone further and have told ourselves that it was mere vanity on our part to think that the corner that we had taken to ourselves had been saved from the general ruin. Indeed we might have questioned whether anybody really agreed with us, or if they were only being polite because 'we meant well according to our lights'. But we were in too desperate a state of mind to trouble with being logical.

In the back of our minds in the previous period there was probably the thought that the work in hand was just to keep the national feeling alive for another generation in the hope that world circumstances during that time might evolve in such a way as to favour Ireland's hopes. And now, according to our 'mystical' doctrine, we may have thought that an elect few would ultimately leaven the whole country.

There was no sign that our friends in Dublin felt the position as we did. It seemed that they would have been quite unconcerned if we marched all our men into the British Army. In desperation we decided that we must do something.

The system of announcing any public event in Dingle was by use of a bellman. He walked through the streets ringing a bell, and announcing this news. I therefore employed him to announce that a public meeting would be held in the Brewery Field on a given night. But the bellman was a 'character'. I happened to be in Dingle while he was doing his work, and I heard him embellishing his announcement with a personal description of myself which had no relation with reality. His glowing description, coupled with the place of the meeting, the 'Brewery' field, leant an air of farce to the whole proposal, and I saw the people listening to his words, convulsed with laughter. I had of course, sent word out to Blythe telling him of the meeting which he must attend.

My bicycle must have been out of order, for I remember that I hired J.H. to drive me into Dingle in his jaunting car. It was very clear that he was not too pleased to be hired for the purpose that I had in mind. He was certainly very careful not to

48

express any approval of my purpose. But half-way in he stopped the car, and took a large sack out of the box, and handing me the reins, told me to hold the horse until he returned as he thought that he had noticed good cabbages in a near-by field. I said that I hadn't known that he held land so far away from home. He told me that that was so, but his own cabbages had failed and 'I never care to sit down to a meal without cabbage on the table'. On this ground he apparently deemed himself quite justified in taking those belonging to a far off neighbour. But he soon returned grumbling under his beard. There was no cabbage there fit to be pulled. For the rest of the journey, while my mind was pre-occupied with the desperate attempt I was making to retrieve some fragment of the Irish nation from the grave, he discoursed upon cabbages and the hardship he suffered when he had to accept meals in which no cabbage figured.

When the people saw us driving through Dingle they all followed to the field. Of course they would have followed us or anybody else who was going to make speeches, for the simple reason that the town provided no other entertainment.

Blythe arrived on his bicycle, but when we looked for a place to make our speeches from, there was none. I decided that we should have to use the jaunting car as a platform, but my driver was very averse to that. However, we just pushed him aside and took possession of the car. We certainly made warlike speeches. I am sure that in our desperate earnestness we were very eloquent. We denounced England as the only enemy Ireland had had since the days of the Vikings, and hailed Germany as the friend for whom Ireland had sought for so long. There was plenty of applause, but that might mean nothing more than that the people were satisfied that we were giving them good entertainment. We were enormously satisfied with our night's work, but our eloquence had not turned my driver's mind from cabbage. He was fairly surly on the way home until he arrived at my gate which was a fairish distance from the house.

'You might get out here Sir,' he said. 'You won't mind the bit of walk up to the house. I want to tie the horse here while I go up to Tom Adams' field. I think I notice that he has good cabbages there. You know I never care to sit down to a meal without cabbage.' I was in no mood to argue with him about the honesty of his method. I got off the car and walked up to the house.

But it appears that irrespective of what effect our oratory had upon the people, we ourselves were much impressed by it, far too much impressed to let it sink beneath the weight of cabbages. It was a short time after this that a case of rifles that we had been awaiting arrived. They came quite openly by rail. We collected them from the station on a Sunday morning after Mass, took them to the Brewery field, where the Volunteers were assembled, and there distributed them. There were not enough to go round, for the news that the rifles had come had produced a maximum attendance. It was the day of the races at Aunascaul, a village about twelve miles away.★

★ *Ed. note:* Ernest Blythe writes as follows about the morning of the Aunascaul races, which took place on 27th September 1914. 'With regard to the I.R.B. oath (see page 50) I can fix the date exactly. It was on the morning of the Volunteer parade to the Aunascaul races or sports on 27th September. The I.R.B. did not become anxious to swear in large numbers of men all over the country until well after Redmond's move in June to grab control of the Volunteers. Early in September I was asked to go down from Kinard to the Tralee-Dingle train on its way westward, and meet Austin Stack whom I knew to be the head of the I.R.B. in Kerry, and whom Sean McDermott had, a week or two earlier, asked me to contact. I got into the carriage with Stack at Lispole and travelled to the next stop—he was a solicitor's clerk on his way to the Petty Sessions at Dingle—and he authorized me to select recruits for the Brotherhood and administer the oath to them. I proceeded to do so, swearing in two or three men at Lispole within the next week or so. On the night before the Aunascaul meeting, Alf Cotton, who was the Volunteer instructor in Tralee and two of the Tralee men arrived in Dingle, having already intimated in advance that they wanted to see Desmond and myself, about something that has escaped my memory.

By the way my opinion is that the rifles for the Dingle Volunteers had arrived at least some days if not a week or two before the Aunascaul meeting. It was possibly the news that the rifles had reached Dingle which brought

When we had given the men a little drill with the rifles—they had already done the drill with sticks—we started off the march to Aunascaul, the men with rifles in front, and the others in the rear. It was a fairly tiring march, for we allowed the minimum halts and rests, being anxious to get to the scene of the races as soon as possible. When we got there the races had already begun, but the sight of a body of men with rifles on their shoulders was so novel that the crowd were even persuaded to turn their attention from the events of the day. This encouraged our new-found arrogance. We suspended the races while we gathered the people around us to listen to our message. Nobody complained of this, the people listened patiently while we

the Tralee men out to see us. I am not sure of my memory on this point. But I am certain that if the rifles were taken off the train that morning neither Desmond nor I was at the station. Desmond and I were with the Tralee men in the house of a Volunteer in the town until the small hours of the Sunday morning. Desmond had been given a key of the Dingle house of Michael O'Kane, who was summering out at Cuan in one of the houses of the coast-guard station. We decided to camp in it. All rooms were securely locked except a bedroom, a sitting-room and the kitchen. We tossed for sleeping places, Desmond and Alf Cotton and the Tralee man whose name I have forgotten got the bed, Billy Mullen got the couch in the sitting-room, and I had to be content with the floor or a bench composed of three or four chairs placed backs against the wall. The bedclothes were divided out amongst us, and we all had a somewhat uncomfortable night, particularly myself. The Tralee man went out in the morning to get something for breakfast. I was left alone in the house with Desmond and had my first chance, since so authorized by Stack, to talk to him about the I.R.B. He readily took the oath and I told him a lot about recent I.R.B. happenings, which years afterwards may have made him think that he had taken the oath earlier than was the case. I mentioned about his having taken the oath to Cotton and the others when they returned with, so far as I remember, nothing but a supply of bread. During our breakfast we all talked about the I.R.B. and particularly about Hobson, whom both Cotton and I knew well, and Desmond was so to speak brought up to date about I.R.B. affairs. I was with Desmond all that morning except when he and the Tralee boys went to Mass. Cotton and I sat talking till they returned.'

From this account it seems likely that the arms had arrived perhaps on the previous Sunday, or several Sundays previously.

unburdened our national souls to them. Blythe was so impressed by the way that they received our doctrine that he even called upon them to raise their hands and declare their allegiance to the independent Irish State. They obeyed without demur.

When the meeting was over, the remaining races had to be run. Nothing short of an earthquake would have been considered a justification for their abandonment. But when the last race was over, the people came about us again. Men with rifles were a novelty, and we were treated as something approaching to heroes. Indeed they wanted to show us their appreciation by 'treating' us in the various pubs. But though we resorted to the pubs, they being the only places of resort, we refused all alcoholic beverage. The men ordering their pints did not resent this, they accepted it as the new policy of national asceticism associated with the leaders of Volunteer companies. It was night-time before we came back. The rifles seemed to grow heavier as we trudged along the heavy road. No doubt many of the men who had been charmed with the honour of bearing a rifle in the morning, would have been glad enough to pass on that honour to their friends who were travelling light. When we got back to Dingle, they were home, but I had the best part of ten miles still to go. But the conviction that the day had been triumphant made that a short journey.

CHAPTER FOUR

The Split in the Volunteers

The sense of utter isolation that had oppressed us was modified by the articles in the little weekly papers that we received. And even the daily papers could not conceal that at least a percentage of the Volunteer leaders and the men were far from agreeing with the doctrine that was implicit in Redmond's speeches in Parliament. At the same time no split had appeared in the organization.*

The long threatened split came soon after that. Mr. Redmond had addressed Volunteers at Aughrim and Woodenbridge in Wicklow and had spoken of defending Ireland in Flanders. It was a clear statement that the duty of Volunteers was to join the British Army. On that the Executive moved, and removed those members who were Redmond nominees. It appeared that Mr. Redmond had underestimated the number of his opponents on the original Executive, and thought that his nominees would be a majority of that body. This error on his part made it a simple matter to remove them. But their removal meant that we were bound to lose their supporters throughout the movement, who were the vast majority. But this did not immediately operate in our district. It could be argued technically that nothing had happened other than that a

* *Ed. note:* It was at this point that the Talbot-Crosbie meeting was described in the original typescript.

number of men had been removed from the Executive, and that their removal had followed necessarily upon the action of the person whose nominee they were, who had tried to use his position to direct the Volunteers into a channel that was not in accordance with the constitution of that body. For the time being, therefore, the most that a Volunteer who followed Redmond could do was to resign as a protest against the exclusion of certain members of the Executive (if they were really members of the Executive, which was argued).

But that situation could not exist for long. The Parliamentary Party proceeded to start a new body to be called the National Volunteers. It was not likely to amount to a great deal, for it would exist for no purpose. Home Rule was shelved until after the War. The Nationalist Party was supporting the British Government strongly in its prosecution of the War. It was illogical for young men to join a quasi-military organization and stay at home, in support of men who made no secret of the fact that they wanted soldiers for foreign battlefields.

But the formation of the new body meant that there was now no reason why a supporter of Redmond should remain a member of our body. And when they went, only a minority would remain. Blythe and I had no objection to the split. For us the Volunteer movement was a vehicle for the dissemination of a national doctrine and an instrument that might ultimately win the greater freedom that Home Rule promised. When war came and Redmond had declared his support of Britain it had seemed to us that there was no further grounds for compromise. We were radically opposed to him and his policy, and any attempt to cover over that radical difference with a poor pretence at unity seemed pointless and misleading to the country. Consequently, when at a Volunteer drill, two of the men (two brothers), voiced their support of Redmond and their disagreement with the 'Executive' I did not try to avoid the issue. On the contrary I invited them to put their case before the men, and I would put mine, and we would take a vote on it. I jumped at this opportunity, as I was satisfied that there was only one other man who would go with them. And these two together with this other man had been trying to oppose me for some time, and I thought it a good opportunity to get rid of them. I also knew that none of the three of them was capable of putting up any real argument.

As I listened to them making their case I felt that they were delivering themselves into my hands. I had chosen to speak last for the purpose of demolishing any case they might try to make. I made my case, put the matter to the vote and out of nearly one hundred men present there were only the three to vote on the opposite side. I was jubilant. While all over the country the vast majority were deserting us for Redmond, I felt that I had succeeded in winning practically the whole organization there. I had never felt that the three men who were going were any asset. One of them, I had heard, was trying to get himself accepted for the R.I.C. And that, according to our doctrine, was the basest treachery conceivable.

But the minority of three were not accepting defeat so easily. When the vote was taken they promptly declared that it meant nothing, as the meeting had not been called for the specific purpose of dealing with that matter. As a matter of fact, the meeting was a particularly good one of active Volunteers. But I was so determined that it should not be said that I was trying to trick the members of the organization, that I invited them to call a meeting for any time and any place. They named an evening about a week ahead, and the place was to be the Temperance Hall. (Incidentally the Hall had little to do with temperance. During its history it had frequently been contaminated by the presence of drunken men.)

I agreed that the meeting should be called, and went home with an easy mind.

On the evening that had been proposed I set off for Dingle. I was still without my bicycle and started off on foot. But when I had gone about three quarters of the way, a well-known Dingle man who was driving a trap offered me a lift which I accepted. He was an influential man who was to be presumed as opposed to my views. I did not doubt that I was going to have an easy victory that night, and if I had, I should have thought the friendly offer of a lift from this man very promising. He had obviously taken a number of drinks, and he was not very articulate. As we drove along I gathered from him that he didn't give a curse about Home Rule or about the language. What interested him was that he held certain land about which there was some controversy, and he was going to hold that against everybody including the devil. At the same time he seemed jubilant about the meeting that was to take place, and made oracular remarks that meant nothing to me about what was going to happen that night.

I took it for granted that when we reached the Hall there would be at most rather more than a hundred Volunteers there to consider the matter that was to be decided. But when we drew near, I saw a seething throng of people trying to enter the already packed building. I had not expected this, but was not so very surprised as I knew of old that the people were always ready to go to any meeting that they thought likely to provide entertainment.

We pushed our way through to the big room upstairs. A number of us tried to get some sort of order and quiet to allow the meeting to proceed, and as soon as comparative order was attained, to my amazement the man who had driven me in got up and proposed a vote of absolute confidence and loyalty to our beloved leader John Redmond. He interwove a good deal of humour, poked at me and 'Mr. Blight' in his speech, though at the same time he gave dark hints that we were in the pay of the 'Keezer'. He gave me a quiet wink when he had finished, but I was now too angry to see any humour. I jumped on to a table to reply to him, but before I could get going, one of the men who had opposed me the week before took hold of me from behind and threw me on to the floor, where I received a few kicks before I was pulled on to my feet again. This did not improve my temper.

A priest who was present, and who had been co-opted on to
56

our local Executive, notwithstanding a rule that had been previously passed that there should be no co-options, now got up and urged that we should go on quietly with our business. And he proposed that the matter we had come to decide should not be dealt with. Instead of taking sides he proposed that we should carry on as we were without any split. But then he went on to state that the split was between the followers of the National Leader on the one side and the followers of three tailors from Tooley Street on the other who called themselves the National Executive.

Under no circumstances could I have allowed that to pass and I certainly was in no mood to be pacific at that moment. I refused the proposal, and asked merely that the Volunteers should consider the matter and decide where they stood.

The priest accepted that.

It was then agreed that he should put the case for the one side and I the opposite case. In spite of my anger I think that I was watchful to see that I should be the last speaker.

The priest then started to make his case. I was astounded. He gave an account of the Volunteers that I had never even heard. Apparently Eoin MacNeill, O'Rahilly and others had nothing to do with starting the movement. They had slipped in in some mysterious way and collared it. But the ever watchful National Leader had taken appropriate steps and appointed his nominees. But those 'Three Tailors from Tooley Street' failed to realize their own utter unimportance and, moved by a sort of madness, had purported to eject the Leader's supporters from the Executive. Naturally the Irish people as one man would follow their own leaders headed by John Redmond who was gloriously leading us along the path to freedom, and was not to be turned from that path by any 'Tooley Street Tailors' or other cranks and soreheads.

I listened patiently to his speech, standing beside him on a large table. I still felt that my task was an easy one. I had only to give a short history of the forming of the Volunteers; refer to the arbitrary way that Redmond had demanded places for his nominees when he saw the dimensions to which the movement had grown; to his failure even to insist that the inadequate measure of Home Rule should be granted, and to his new doctrine that it was the duty of Irishmen to go out and fight for England in Flanders. I stepped forward to smash the pitiful case that had been made. But at the same time, a powerful man jumped up on the table. He also appeared to have had a few drinks. 'Friends', he said, 'I have only two words to say.' Of course, the agreement that had been come to was that the only two speakers should be the priest and myself. But I was prepared to assent to this breach of the agreement, as I only wanted to be the last to speak, and I thought I was very cleverly managing to achieve that plan. I stepped back to let the newcomer have his say. But he actually said four words. They were 'Down with the traitor', and as he said them he brought his fist round into my eye with such force that he lifted me from the table and threw me into the corner unconscious.

It must have been some time after that before I opened the other eye and looked round, for the room was now practically empty save for a few friends, one of whom was fanning me to bring me back to consciousness. I could hear cheering and shouting in the street. Finally I was assisted out of the hall, and on my almost ten miles walk home. The crushing speech that I had made in my mind was never delivered.

After that I had to remain in bed for a week. Indeed I might have stayed there longer but during the week a couple of men came out from Dingle to tell me that there was to be a meeting of the local Executive on a certain night and that at all costs I must be there. I therefore arranged that the cabbage-loving J.H. would bring his car to drive me in. The priest who had made the speech the week before was present and he showed every sign of friendliness, as though to make amends. But I merely told him that he had no right to be present as co-opted members had been expressly barred. The others present tried to get me not to make this objection, but the priest merely asked them if what I stated was correct and they had to agree that it was so. He withdrew later. When I went out into the town and talked to people I found that everybody had known that the previous week's meeting had been organized against me. I had remained in ignorance because I lived so far from the town. The man who organized the trouble had gone round boasting that they would 'wipe the floor' with me, and after it was over he was able to point out that his promise had been fulfilled very literally. Most people felt that I had been treated shamefully and were ready to condemn the man who struck me, but I felt that there was something to be said for the fact that he had come out quite openly, while the man who had arranged the whole thing had remained carefully in the background. Apparently he thought that I remained quite unaware of his activities, as some years later when the position in the country had quite changed, and we were the dominant party, I travelled in the train from Tralee to Dingle with him, and he insisted on telling me how much he had admired me during that early time. He depicted himself as my most sincere but most unobtrusive supporter during that time. I did not hint that I knew anything to the contrary. He was obviously enjoying 'bluffing' me, and I did not spoil his enjoyment.

As soon as my eye was moderately open again I summoned Volunteers for drill. Twenty-three turned up. I remember feeling that the majority came principally as a 'mark of sympathy'. The fewness of their number reacted upon them. They felt that they were no longer part of a great national movement. They saw little to give them encouragement or enthusiasm. But I announced that drills would be held regularly as before, and tried to appear as though the absence of eighty per cent of the number we had been used to was unnoticeable.

Previously a certain enthusiasm had flowed from the knowledge that they were participating in a big movement, that their organization was recognized as the most significant in the country. The large space in the newspapers given up to reports of Volunteer activities created in their minds a sense of solidarity with their comrades all over the country. Now they had to adjust their minds to the new situation in which they were associated with a movement that was small and that seemed to be running counter to the whole mind of the country. We were apparently a minority in our own district, and yet it seemed that we were relatively stronger there than in any other part of the country. Nevertheless, the twenty-three increased again in numbers, though very slowly.

Meanwhile, arrangements were made for a convention in Dublin of the organization in its new and very much contracted (or as we should have said, very much purified) condition. It was not difficult for Blythe and me to get our respective units to appoint us as delegates especially as we were to pay our own expenses. And a third delegate also came from that area. He was a man who belonged to the district in the West, but who had been in Dublin for a long time as an Irish teacher. He was well known in certain circles in Dublin as he had written Irish columns for weekly papers. He was also well known there in West Kerry, but this was more unfortunate than otherwise, as the people had sat in judgment on him and their verdict was not lenient. He had come to some of our meetings in that part when speeches were to be made and had spoken with considerable eloquence in beautiful Irish. He was a popular speaker just for that reason, but the people indicated in conversation that they had no illusions that he would put his fine sentiments into practice involving loss or risk to himself. Indeed they habitually referred to him by a very offensive nickname which summed up their estimate of him. He had persuaded the men in his own district to subscribe for his expenses as a delegate to the Convention.

We set off for Dublin very happily. It was more than pleasant to be going to a gathering in the capital in which all those present would be at one with our ideas. Probably we felt in need of some such event to hearten and to cheer us, but to ourselves we represented it that we should be able to bring back a real assurance to our men that in all parts of the country there were others sharing their doctrine and working the same way for the same end.

We were particularly cheered when, after the train had stopped at Mallow Junction two men got in, one wearing a bowler hat and consequently not looking in the least like a Volunteer, while the other not only had the mark of the 'delegate' written all over him, but eyed us, as though he realized that we were on the same errand as himself. Finally he came over to us and said, 'I think ye must be on the same mission as myself'. We replied that we were going to the Convention of the Irish Volunteers. He said that he also was a delegate. And then in a confidential whisper he told us that the other man was also coming. He (the speaker) had got his people to nominate this man. He was a recent convert, and didn't understand the matter very well. Indeed he seemed to regard him as a convert not too well established in the faith. But, he continued, he was important. He had 'six hundred pounds of his own'. It was all important that he should be encouraged to continue in the right national path, as it would have a good effect on his whole district, and it was therefore to be hoped that we would encourage him.

He then brought his friend along, and our conversation was directed to inspiring him with a reinforced ardour in the cause. We certainly did our best, in spite of the fact that the bowler hat worn on the back of his head, maintained an impression in our minds that his mental equipment was so limited that the doctrine could only be propounded to him in a primer form.

But just as we were becoming exhausted from the effort, our Irish speaking colleague from the West, who had been showing signs of a certain restlessness, announced that there was a bar on the train and he thought it would be a good idea to retire there for a drink. At last the light of enthusiasm came into the eyes of the man with the bowler hat. He jumped to his feet at the suggestion. The other man who had joined us at Mallow looked doubtfully at Blythe and me. We indicated that though we did not propose retiring to the bar ourselves we were making no objection to others doing so. Whereupon the three of them hastily disappeared. They came back to us from time to time during the rest of the journey, but never to stay long. Our Western colleague who had told us earlier that he had asked from his supporters only enough money to pay his fare and lodgings at a common lodging house for the two nights that he would have to stay in Dublin seemed to have taken such a fancy to his two boon companions that in our presence he got from them the name of the hotel they would be staying at. We were a little worried as we felt partly responsible for his behaviour, and already we had a shrewd suspicion that the liquid source of his present happiness was being paid for by the two newcomers. But we had no opportunity of conveying any word of caution to them behind his back.

As usual, when I arrived in Dublin, I stayed with O'Rahilly. His optimism and his enthusiasm were refreshing and soon dissipated any discouragement that might have been lurking at the back of my head. The movement had been steadily pushing ahead ever since the split. Germany was certain to smash England. Before the War was over, forces would be landed in Ireland, and we should co-operate with them. As a result of the war this Irish nation that had been no more than a dream for so long would be a reality. It was all too wonderful to be believed. But it was wonderful to get such assurances here at the very centre of things.

The Convention itself should have been as tedious as such gatherings usually are. There was a resolution proposed by O'Rahilly which I seconded by arrangement with him to the effect that the Irish words 'Fianna Fail' should be officially recognized as equivalent to the English words 'Irish Volunteers'. The resolution was so phrased in order that it would not exclude the name 'Oglaigh na h-Eireann' which was already established as the Irish name of the movement. It was innocuous enough, but it was hotly contested by Mr. Eamon Ceannt, who had originally suggested 'Oglaigh na h-Eireann'. In the end O'Rahilly's proposition was agreed to. Other resolutions of the same importance, or lack of importance were put forward and argued, and finally accepted or rejected. But even these things could not damp the general atmosphere of enthusiastic hope that prevailed.

During our time in Dublin we saw most of our friends in the movement there, and others whom we had not met before but whose names were familiar to us. Of course I could not miss the opportunity to go and see Arthur Griffith whom I had admired and revered since I was a boy. I think that he was just bringing out a new paper. Some such thing was happening and a number of his friends were foregathered for the event. It was a joy to see that he knew me immediately I went in and treated me as a friend. During that evening I felt that our relationship was transformed and that a mutual personal affection subsisted between us.

But in spite of our happiness in Dublin it never occurred to Blythe or to me to extend our stay there. We had come up for a purpose and once that was done, we went back. We hoped to see our Western colleague at the station but he did not turn up. Indeed it was probably a couple of weeks before he reappeared. But on the train we saw the two friends we had made at Mallow. They also were anxious to know what had happened to our friend. He had borrowed some money from them (or rather from the man with the bowler hat). He had stayed at their hotel and when they were leaving they found that they were charged with his bill. The enthusiast was worried about this, not because of the monetary loss, but he was afraid that it might have a bad effect upon his friend with the bowler hat. His still incomplete faith might go to pieces on that rock.

We had not been back long when Blythe came to tell us that he had been called to Dublin to become an organizer for the movement. As a matter of fact, he explained, although he was officially being employed by the Volunteer organization it was really being arranged by the headquarters of the I.R.B. He was to organize Volunteers certainly, but behind that he was

63

to recruit for the I.R.B. We knew that the Central Council of the I.R.B. had decided that there was to be a Rising during the war, but this news that Blythe had gave a greater reality to that decision. It meant that they had not merely passed a sort of pious resolution, but were already taking steps to put that resolution into effect.

Originally Blythe had intended to stay for at least two years labouring on a farm and absorbing a knowledge of Irish. But at that time no one had foreseen the rapid developments that had subsequently taken place. He was now going off to Dublin, and from there to various parts of the country. There was a great thrill in his news, but it also brought a sense of desolation. We had worked together during all that time. We were entirely at one. Now he was going away, and I was to be left to carry on alone. Even the implication that his appointment meant that what we had been doing had not passed unnoticed and unappreciated by the leaders of the movement in Dublin, could not obliterate the sense of impotent loneliness that his departure also brought.

I saw that the absence of Blythe, together with the whole situation as it then stood, meant that I should have to be more active if anything.* For instance it meant that when one of us was required at some distant place I should always have to go. Thus on one occasion I got a telegram from the O'Rahilly saying that he was announced to speak in Castleisland and was unable to go and that I must take his place. It meant that I should have to set out immediately, and just at that moment there was no ready money in the house. The only thing to do was to set off for Dingle and borrow what it would cost from someone there. The only possible lender I could think of approaching was a shop-keeper whom I knew rather well, but I felt that it was a humiliating thing to have to ask for a loan, and as I went in I was turning over various ways of broaching my request to him. When I finally entered the shop I still

* *Ed. note:* It was during this period that Mabel FitzGerald initiated the correspondence with George Bernard Shaw which is printed in an Appendix.

had no idea of what I was going to say to him, and I just talked of general topics while I tried to screw up my courage to mention the matter that was on my mind. It seemed almost miraculous when he suddenly said 'By the way I owe you a pound, I should have given it to you long ago but it went out of my mind. Why didn't you remind me?'

It had certainly gone out of my mind also. I thought at first that he must have made a mistake. Then he recalled the circumstances to me, and I remembered, and pocketed the dirty pound note that he passed over to me. I left that shop with a light heart, and made off for the station.

I had to stay that night in Tralee, and spent the evening with Volunteers there. They were due to be present at the meeting the next day; those who were equipped with rifles were to parade with them.

In Castleisland there was a platform erected for the meeting as is the custom, and as we approached that platform, police advanced and lined themselves around it so that the Volunteers and the ordinary people had to listen to us speaking over the policemen's heads, but a body of armed Volunteers came on the platform with us as a bodyguard. It was a very large meeting, in fact it was the largest Irish Volunteer meeting that had been held in the country since the split. I threw discretion to the winds in my speech and said very severe things about those police who as servants of the British Government could dictate to Irish people in Ireland. What else I said I don't remember, but when the meeting was over I was told that I was due to be arrested and therefore the armed bodyguard would remain with me and escort me back to Tralee. It seemed to be regarded as all important that I should be got back to Tralee safe and sound, though nobody seemed to have thought about what was to happen when we got there and the armed men went home to their beds. I was escorted to the place I was to stay at in Tralee and there my guards said good-bye and went home, and when I got inside and looked out of the window I saw police stationed outside the house. But the next morning early I got up and caught the morning train to Dingle and was not interfered with. I had in fact by that time got used to being accompanied by police. Whenever I went into Dingle I was picked up by a policeman or two and they kept beside me as long as I stayed in the town; so closely beside me that if I met a man in the street and spoke to him, I had to whisper my remarks if they were not to be overheard by the uniformed man beside me. The chief annoyance that this caused me was the fact that when the children saw me walking about with the policeman at my hotel or at my side they followed us about, so that I had the embarrassment of going about the town followed by a troop of shouting children.

Also when I went to Tralee I was picked up by a detective there who remained with me until I caught the train back. There was only one occasion when this was awkward and that was when I had gone there to attend a meeting that was supposed to be very secret. The difficulty was finally solved by going into a house that had a back door leading on to another street. I came out of the back door and ran to the place of the meeting and got there before my shadow had picked me up again.

CHAPTER FIVE

Expelled to Wicklow

So it was until towards the end of January 1915. Then one morning as I sat down to breakfast I looked out and saw that policemen with carbines were stationed about the lawn. At the same moment the maid came in to tell me that the District Inspector wanted to see me. I found him in another room. He was quite friendly in his demeanour and handed me a notice saying that I was to give up my house within a month, and I myself was to leave Kerry within six days and not enter it again, and also that thereafter I was not to reside in a prohibited area. I inquired what were and what were not prohibited areas, but he had no information on that matter. I could go to Dublin he said, and when I got there I should be informed as to what places were open to me for residence.

I telegraphed to Dublin to Volunteer Headquarters for instructions and was told to obey the order. I went in to Dingle and gathered the Volunteers together (their number had now improved so that at that last meeting I think rather more than eighty turned up). I told them what had happened; used it to illustrate how utterly unfree our country was when an outside government could give such orders to Irishmen in Ireland and enforce them. I appointed a man in charge, and said goodbye.

Cathal Brugha and Austin Stack were at the station in Tralee when we arrived. It was pleasant to find friends waiting there as well as detectives. I really expected that Cathal Brugha, being from the very centre of things in Dublin, would be able to make an authoritative statement on effective steps to be taken in relation to such arbitrary acts by the British Government. But instead of that he was sympathetic with me and my family on the annoyance that was caused to us. He seemed just to accept it as a fact that the British Government could tell us to get out of our house and dictate as to where we should live, and, accepting that as a fact, he was concerned to help us in that situation. I was certainly very conscious of the inconvenience that the order had imposed upon us, but I did not regard it as a tragedy. In fact I had laughed uproariously when the owner of the jaunting car had come to drive me into Dingle that morning, and had arrived with a face of infinite gloom, reiterating while he waited for us to get our things on to the car, that he always looked on an eviction as worse than a death.

Once the headquarter's message had come that I was to obey the order, I had accepted the position. In fact I was quite interested in the thought of where we were to live. Apparently I regarded it as most important that I should live in a place where the surrounding country was beautiful. Assuming that I should not be allowed to live in Dublin, I was wondering if Wicklow would be closed to me, for after Kerry, it seemed to me that the most beautiful, or as I might say 'sympathetic' countryside would be in that county.

The sympathy my friends gave me in Tralee was most welcome. I had a hunted feeling, and in that condition it was heart-warming to feel that one had friends who agreed with one's actions and realized to the full, and perhaps beyond it, the awkwardnesses that one's actions had produced. It was also very flattering to be recognized as one who was suffering for the cause, and gratifying to have that suffering rather exaggerated. But while I had used the order given to me by the British Authorities in Dingle to show how unfree we really were, I quite unreasonably half hoped that the leaders in and from

68

Dublin, would show signs that we were not so unfree after all, and that somehow we had power to make British orders ineffective in Ireland.

But that was only a half hope lurking in the back of my mind. When I sat down to think the matter over I knew that the leaders in Dublin were only leaders of people like myself, and that those people were few, a minority that could not make itself heard by the country as a whole. It had been the consciousness of the remoteness of my own district that had induced the feeling that some real power existed in the centre of the movement.

O'Rahilly met us in Dublin, and nobody who saw us that night could have thought that we were suffering affliction 'worse than a death'. It was really a joyous gathering of friends. When a police official came with a list of the 'prohibited places', we treated it as a great joke that most places in Ireland seemed to be 'prohibited'. We argued jubilantly that that meant that the British had to recognize that the most of Ireland was dangerous because the people were, or could be made to be, hostile to them. The D.I. in Dingle had prepared me for the news that I should not be allowed to live in Dublin, and the document brought that night revealed that Wicklow County from Bray to within twenty miles of Arklow Post Office was open to me. That meant that I could live in the place that I had already selected in my mind.

My wife could only stay a short time in Dublin as she had to get back to Kerry to get packed and moved with all our household goods. But during those few days we saw all our friends, and we felt that we were being fêted as heroes, as sufferers for the cause. Also O'Rahilly drove us out around the parts of Wicklow that were open to us, and though it was the month of January it was clear that the prerequisite of naturally beautiful countryside was abundantly fulfilled.

While in Dublin I visited in their homes the members of the Executive whom I knew. Blythe happened to be there at that time, and of course we spent a good deal of time together. In the Volunteer Offices we visited the Secretary of the Volunteers,★ who was also an office holder in the I.R.B. He was an old friend of Blythe, and Blythe always spoke of him with great respect. I knew him also, but not as Blythe did. Indeed I had met him through Blythe. I expected that as my other friends had done he would greet us both warmly, Blythe as an old and loyal friend, and me as one who was suffering for the cause. But when we went into his office, he looked up from what he was writing and nodded, and then continued writing as though we were not there. I could understand that he might just be finishing a sentence or a letter, that would only take him a minute or so, but he continued writing and disregarding us for an unconscionable time, in a way that seemed to me distinctly offensive and ill-mannered. Especially as it seemed that what he was writing must be something of no importance. I whispered to Blythe once or twice that we might just as well go on about our business, but he sat stolidly on. At last when I began to make a move to go, our host put down his pen and turned to us quite genially. In fact we talked over many things before I got to the business of my visit. It is true that he did not pour out sympathy with me for the way I had been treated by the English. That, as well as everything else that had happened and was happening was good for the cause. He spoke as though we (and particularly he) controlled enormous (though very hidden) power. One gathered that he knew all that was to be known about the war and how it was going to develop. And with that vast knowledge he looked to the immediate future with an absolutely equable mind.

'Is it certain that Germany would win?' I asked.

'Absolutely certain.' He was even prepared to demonstrate that it was militarily necessary and inevitable.

'Is it definitely decided that we should rise while the war was on?'

'Definitely settled.'

His whole tone and manner also definitely assured me that

★ *Ed. note:* Bulmer Hobson.

there would be no fear that the War would end suddenly and unexpectedly before we had struck a blow. I could not question him on such matters, as apparently he was deep in the confidence of the German leaders, and it would look as though I doubted that or were asking him to betray their confidence.

I then reminded him that I was going to live in Bray, was there a company of Volunteers there?

No there was not. But there was a circle of the I.R.B.

Would I be put in touch with them?

He would see to that.

I supposed that I should set about organizing a company when I settled in Bray.

Yes, I should, and, as I knew, an order had gone out to all circles of the I.R.B. that their members were to become Volunteers, so I should have the local members of that body as a nucleus to start from.

In any case would I be kept in touch with headquarters and be duly notified when the Rising was to take place?

I need not worry about that. He would see to it.

All this wiped out the effect of the reception he had given us when we arrived. Nevertheless, when we got outside I hastened to tell Blythe what I thought of the bad manners he had shown us. But Blythe only laughed. That was just to impress you he said. That is his way. We both laughed at it as an amiable foible, but I still maintained that it was damn bad manners, and told Blythe that he should make an opportunity to point out to his friend that it might not always have the effect that he expected.

With these points cleared up it was my immediate task to find the house in which we were to live, as within a fortnight railway trucks with our furniture would arrive at Bray. I took lodgings at Bray and spent my days in looking for a house. During those days I walked the whole countryside, and there were times when I thought that an available and suitable house did not exist. It also seemed to me that if people knew why I was looking for a house they would be horrified at the very thought of such a man as I entering under any roof that belonged to them. When I stated that I could not take any house that was across the boundary of Dublin County they assumed that I was a Government official whose appointment stipulated that he must live in Wicklow County. When I interviewed anyone who might conceivably have a house to let, there was inevitably a general conversation which brought in the War, and the owner of the possible house would always break out into denunciations of the Germans and particularly of that fountain of all evil, the 'Kayser'.

It was clear that the landlady from whom I had taken lodgings was anxious to know who and what I was. Also that I had impressed her as a very respectable person. She was so kind and friendly that I rather dreaded telling her the awful truth, but it had to be done, as the police would be around. For one of the conditions imposed upon me in the later order that I had received was that I must notify my place of residence to the police, and not reside outside it without previous notice to them.

It was within a day or two of my arrival that she came in with a rather awestruck face to tell me that the police sergeant wanted to see me. He came in with, I think a new order. That may have been the one which notified me that not only must I not reside in a prohibited area, but also that I must not enter a prohibited area. When he had gone, the landlady in her conversation showed that she assumed that I must be a new D.I. for the district. She made this so clear, that it meant that if I did not deny it, she would feel that I had really assented to it. I braced myself, and made a clean breast of it. But far from giving me notice on the spot, she began to be enthusiastic. Her family had always been strong nationalists. Her mother had always felt that the one disgrace that could not be overcome was that any son of hers should be a robber or join the British Army. That made things easier.

Mr. Griffith in Dublin had told me of a man he knew in Bray who had been a Sinn Feiner for a long time, and had advised me to look him up. He was a civil servant, but all enthusiasm for the Volunteers, and he received me with open arms with my two credentials that I was a friend of Griffith and that the British Government had driven me from my home. I looked to him to give me advice as to men who would be likely to join the Volunteers when I formed a company in the district. He was more than willing to assist in any way he could. He had lived there for years and knew all about everybody. He would mention a name and then give a rapid account of its owner which was intensely amusing, but was far from suggesting that he or any of them were potential Volunteers. Indeed I gathered that I might practically rule out anybody who wore a collar or tie, and most of the others.

One evening when I was in my sitting-room in my lodgings the landlady, who was still convinced of my eminent respectability notwithstanding what she knew about me, came in with rather horrified eyes to tell me that there were two men to see me. But before I could ask who they were, they appeared behind her. They came forward and announced themselves as officers of the I.R.B. in the area. I was of course delighted to see them, and only regretted that they came accompanied by such a strong odour of alcohol. I wanted to talk business with them, but they seemed only to want to tell me of the veneration amounting to awe with which they looked upon a patriot against whom the ever-perfidious enemy had struck with all his venom. I should have appreciated this more if they had not such difficulty in making it articulate.

I asked when and where the circle met.

They seemed rather vague about that, but told me to lift up my heart, for they and the other members were all united in their admiration of me.

I said I required to know, as I supposed that I should attend the meeting.

That proposal seemed rather to shock them. They said there was certainly no need for me to attend. Everybody knew that I was staunch. And the British Government had marked me down. Anybody so marked down was spied upon by the peelers. A man such as I was such a danger to the accursed Empire that their agents would never leave me out of their sight. There would be no need for me to attend any meetings. The police would follow me, and it would only make them the more venomous against me.

I assured them that I was prepared for the worst that England could do, and was ready to attend any meeting that they cared to tell me of.

They, on their side refused to let me sacrifice myself. As I seemed to be getting nowhere on that line, I asked how many members they had. They both replied at once naming a number, but they did not name the same number. But that was unimportant, except as I pointed out to them, that I was starting a company of Volunteers in that district, and as they knew the Supreme Council had issued an order that all members of the organization should join the Volunteers, it would be useful for me to know so that I could be guaranteed that their full membership would come to the meeting that I would call.

They did not seem to be quite sure as to whether they had heard of any such order. I said in any case it didn't matter whether or not the order had been received by their circle, obviously every member would recognize it as his duty to join the company that I proposed to form.

They did not seem very convinced about that, but agreed rather inarticulately, and went on to assert the enormous respect they felt for a man like me and what an honour it was to them to be in my presence. Whenever their eloquence on this topic showed signs of becoming too exalted, I punctured it by telling how splendid it was that I could be certain from their noble sentiments that they would be at all meetings and drills inspiring others with a like ardour. When they were gone the landlady came in to discuss them. She had a most mordant sense of humour.

As soon as we were settled in a house, I got to work to form a company. We began with a few, and new recruits

appeared from time to time. We could not afford to take anything so ambitious as a hall, and, in fact we did not need it for
the number we had. Only a very small proportion of the
population could have been aware that there was such a thing
as a Volunteer company.

But now I was in constant touch with headquarters. I was not
allowed to enter Dublin, certainly, but friends, who were heart
and soul in the movement were constantly coming out to us.
There was never a week-end that there were not some staying
with us. Consequently we were well fed, not only with information on every development, but also with every item of
rumour and gossip. And as I was an honorary organizer for
Wicklow, I used to go off on week-days cycling through the
country and if I failed to get supporters into my net, I at least had
the joy of exploring new country whose beauty enthralled me.

I most rigidly obeyed the order that I had received from the
police as far as the Dublin direction was concerned, but I was
not so conscientious in the other directions. I certainly did not
take a map to measure what places were within twenty miles
of Arklow Post Office. But I was saved from disobeying too
flagrantly by the limits that one could do in a day on a bicycle,
when one had to stop in every place on the road to see if by
any chance there was a possible supporter to be won there.

When the summer came I disregarded the order to the
extent of renting a cottage at Kilmalin near the mountains and
going to live there without permission of the police. The day
after I took up residence there a sergeant called to inform me
that what I had done contravened the order, but that I should
be allowed to stay there for the time that I had arranged.

As our time there coincided with the holiday period, the
cottage was crowded the whole time. The Volunteers had
decided to run training camps, and the first of these was to be
pitched in Wicklow moving from place to place. They were
due to pass our house on the way, and naturally the leaders
would call in. But the first notification that the Volunteers
were arriving was that a man was brought in injured by a fall

75

from his bicycle. The road leading to Kilmalin from Dublin is a particularly dangerous one and just before reaching where we lived was one place appropriately called the Devil's Elbow. The road is a steep hill, with zigzag bends. It was there that the Volunteer had met with the accident. But before we had finished dressing his wounds another was brought in and then another. They had had similar accidents at the same spot. This had all made for delay and the injured men had also injured their bicycles, so it was decided to pitch the camp in the field behind our house.

In West Kerry I had, of course, known my men intimately. But since I had left that part, I had only met the men when they turned up for drill. So the event of the camp really gave me my first chance of getting into contact with the men. But even this was not a very close contact with any except those who were in charge of them. When the day's work of the camp was done these usually came into the house and spent the remainder of the evening there. On these occasions they talked of the coming 'scrap' lightheartedly as an exciting event to be looked forward to. But I found this conversation rather depressing. They seemed to foresee it as a sort of prolonged and widespread camp life, in which they would be commanding a countryside and occasionally shooting at the enemy. The initial act of rising in arms, with its enormous responsibility was lightly passed over, the outcome, insofar as it was referred to, was presupposed as a complete military victory. In a general way the presence of German forces was presumed. But all other aspects and possibilities were blandly ignored. It was not thought necessary to point to any existing data that gave grounds for assuming that the German forces would be there. There was no discussion as to whether the Rising should take place in the absence of such help, and it would have been the worst of bad taste to consider for a moment the possibility of defeat and the fate that might then await those who had not already been killed in the fight.

When the camp moved on to Glencree I accompanied it to

see it installed there. The only ground made available for it was on the steep slope of a hill. The tents were wigwam tents just large enough for three men to lie in side by side. I shared a tent with the Commandant and the Vice-Commandant, and I chose to sleep in the middle that my comrades might shelter me from draughts on either side. But we lay on a ground sheet, and the slope of the hill and the fact that I was just opposite the entrance to the tent, meant that constantly during the night I slid until I was outside the tent and had to get up and return to its shelter. Although it was the month of June or July, the nights were bitterly cold. I admired the cheeriness of the men who regarded it all as a splendid holiday. Personally I was very glad that I was only to stay for two nights and then to return and to spend my nights in a house.

The camp then moved on farther into Wicklow. It was due to pass by our house at the end and to be pitched in our field for the very last night. But within a couple of days we were astounded to see the men on bicycles arriving back in our field. The reason was that in other places when, with great difficulty, they got permission to erect the tents on someone's land the local police would call on the owner and have a talk with him, as a result of which, the owner would then demand that they leave his land. Under the circumstances they decided that it would be best to come back to the only bit of comparatively level ground that they had met with and whose owner would welcome them.

During that summer Blythe and one or two others had been given an order by the police commanding them to leave Ireland. This they refused to obey and were soon arrested and tried and sentenced to three months' imprisonment. At their trial they had been defended and the defence had disturbed me, as it was directed to win an acquittal by representing the accused as being most innocent of any action or attitude of mind that was incompatible with their being good Irish subjects of the British Government.

When Blythe came after his release he gave a most detailed account of the prison régime, which had a particular interest, as I had no idea what prison conditions were like, and at the same time had to recognize that I might have to face them at any time. I found his story most reassuring. His account of the diet was the most depressing part of his story, for I knew myself to be difficult with regard to food, there were so many things that I simply could not eat. This had been in my mind for some time, for quite apart from the prospect of prison, I assumed that when the Rising would take place and we should be scattered about the country, we should have to be content with whatever food was available. For instance I thought that we might have no other means of sustenance than raw potatoes dug out of the fields. I felt that I would be useless in those circumstances, if I did not get some training beforehand to accustom me to a crude diet. The account that Blythe gave seemed to me to represent something of such a training.

I told Blythe what I felt about the defence that had been made at his trial, and he entirely agreed with me. He told me that he had agreed to a defence, but that as the lawyer proceeded with it, he realized that it was all wrong. My line was that if one took certain action to put a doctrine of nationalism before the Irish people one had to recognize that the probability was that that would lead to gaol. Having done that and been arrested it was clear that the only question that would be decided was the amount of imprisonment to be allotted. To have a lawyer explaining that one did not mean what one said, and then to get three months, meant that one's whole course of action had been silly. It meant that one got three months in gaol for nothing. Whereas if one were really convinced that what had been done or said was for the national good, and then pay for it with a longer term of imprisonment, one might at least feel that the credit side of national good went some way to balance the debit side of imprisonment.

I was glad to have Blythe agreeing with my views on this point, for I felt that I might at any time be in a similar position and would have to decide upon my own course of action.

Tommy MacDonagh who was a member of the Executive of the Volunteers took his holiday that year in Greystones. That was only five miles from Bray and within my non-prohibited area. Naturally I took that opportunity to have talks with him, or rather I should say listen to him talking for he allowed very few breaks in his conversation. Apparently I referred to the training camp and my experience with it. But he waved such projects away as meaningless. The man who had promoted the camps had been very insistent upon them and had therefore been allowed to go ahead, rather on the grounds that they would do no harm, rather than that they would serve any useful purpose.

'His mind runs on country fighting, taking cover behind hedges and so forth,' said Tommy. 'But that all means nothing. It would really be much more useful to be getting such things as the keys of buildings in Dublin or instruction in street fighting.'

I saw from this that he was thinking of the fight as rather concentrated in Dublin, and I asked how we were to stand up to artillery. If we were in buildings in Dublin, surely we could be shelled from land or from sea. If British warships lay off the coast and just dropped shells upon us I didn't see that we could do much against them.

But he waved all that on one side. He was not very explicit as to why that was not likely to happen, but he suggested that the British would not shell the city, as by doing so they would be injuring their own supporters.

It seemed to me that the British were at least convinced that they were now fighting for their existence as an Empire, while we should be fighting to drive them completely out of Ireland. To expect them to accept defeat rather than shell Dublin seemed to me fantastic. But MacDonagh smiled tolerantly at my objections and again reassured me that everything was quite all right, Dublin would not be bombarded. One could not stand up against his cheery optimism. In a childlike way I felt that he must have grounds for his hopes that he had not communicated to me. But, as against that, on later reflection the assumption that we should be allowed to take possession of our country merely because the British would be too considerate to make use of the power that they undoubtedly possessed had a necessarily depressing effect.

The reaction of the majority of the Irish people after the declaration of war had filled me with the conviction that we had reached a point where the Irish people were accepting completely their absorption by the British. Up to then there was still hope that the Irish people were merely recognizing the material fact that the British held their country with a stronger power than they could hope to overcome until circumstances changed. But now it was generally assumed that we must do all possible to maintain the power, even to the extent of giving Irish lives for that purpose. Once that point of view was established, it would be futile to talk of ourselves other than as the inhabitants of that part of England that used to be called Ireland. In that state of mind I had decided that extreme action must be taken if even the lukewarm watered down regionalistic nationalism that had maintained a moribund life up to that time was to be maintained. The fact that England was now at grips with a power comparable with herself offered some prospect for an armed Rising in conjunction with that power. But now the War had been going on for a year and though we read into every item of war news the promise of British defeat, when I was completely honest with myself I had to recognize that to say the least that was not by any means certain. So far, in any case, the War had not developed in such a way as would allow the Germans to bring their ships of troops and equipment to Ireland by overcoming British opposition on the route. I hung upon the words of members of the Executive and all others who I thought might have information that I did not possess, seeking material to feed optimism. But they never seemed to have information that I could build great hopes upon.

To do nothing seemed to be to accept the final abandonment of all Ireland's dreams. And the alternative was to sanction the leading out of young men upon a course which meant that those who were not so fortunate as to be shot during the struggle, would only have to face the firing squad or the gallows immediately after the defeat.

With the consciousness of this alternative in the back of my mind I could not take joy in those lighthearted conversations of some of my friends about the 'scrap' that was to come off, and I could not accept their impatience for that moment to arrive. I scanned the war news in the papers to see if there were signs of developments that promised a condition in which we could take up arms with a fair certainty of success. But those developments did not appear, although there was always the hope that they were merely postponed. We must work on, so as to be ready when and if that moment should arrive, but I had to admit to myself that it had not arrived yet. There was no moment past or present when I could have lightheartedly called upon men to take up their arms and march to victory.

These gloomy views were in the depths of my mind rather than at the surface. I am quite sure that when they tended to come to the surface I discouraged them as far as possible. But in any case I should not have felt that we should cease to develop the Volunteer movement. In fact, if we had won a majority of the people to support that organization I might have felt that there was no absolute need to rise in arms, for it implied a certain doctrine of nationalism. If a majority of the people affirmed our right to independence, and were only withheld from seizing that right by the knowledge of the overwhelming material forces against us, then one might have assumed that we were only waiting for the opportune moment. But knowing that we were only a very small minority it seemed that the work to hand was to win as many to our ranks as possible. To increase our numbers was at least to accomplish something, independent of the consideration of improving our strength for armed conflict. What was oppressive was that whatever progress we made in gaining recruits still left it abundantly certain that no matter how long the War might reasonably last, we should still be a small minority when it was over and consequently powerless, unless we accomplished something during the War. And that 'something' meant a Rising, and that Rising required a development in the War which certainly might come, but which was far from being inevitable.

I continued to try to find men in Wicklow who would work to get Volunteer companies formed in their districts, without any marked success, though apparently I expected so little that I would come home quite elated if I had found a man here and there who showed willingness to co-operate in the work. But even this was rare. There was even a certain amount of satisfaction in meeting a man who was definitely opposed if it led to an argument in the presence of young men, for one always felt that some of them might be impressed by the case made. What was utterly disheartening was the deadly rebuff. I remember one such instance that made me feel humiliated every time it came back to my mind. I was told that the one place to get the men in Enniskerry gathered together was in the library at night. It was customary to gather there and play cards. I arranged that Eimar O'Duffy, who had been the Vice-Commandant of the Camp, and another young man who was well up in drill would accompany me. The other young man came in Volunteer uniform. We went to the library and found it full of men the majority of whom were young. They were deep in a game of cards. I had no hesitation in asking that they would listen to what we had to say. A game of cards seemed grotesquely unimportant at that moment of Ireland's history. Very agreeably they put their cards down on the table face downwards and sat back to listen. I harangued them with great fervour and moved by my own eloquence I pointed out to the young men the wonderful opportunity they now had to take up arms in Ireland's service and thus unite themselves with the glorious tradition of Ireland's struggle. They listened attentively. In conclusion I said that we were willing to come regularly on whatever evenings suited them to drill them in preparation for the service that I proposed to them. I invited them to state what arrangements they would like made. When I had finished there was dead silence. They seemed uncertain as to whether I really had finished, and loath to interrupt me. Then they looked from one to another, and as it was clear that we were then waiting for a response from them, one man turned to another and said, 'I think it was your play, Jim,' and another picking up his hand of cards asked what had been trumps. Then the play began again as though we were not there. We waited helplessly for a minute or so, and then saw that there was nothing to do but to go on our way. We were bitterly angry, but they had not asked us to come, they had listened to us as long as we spoke, and they simply were not interested, and were certainly not sufficiently moved to want to seize the opportunity offered to them to die in Ireland's service.

CHAPTER SIX

Arrest, trial and imprisonment

Meanwhile, the company in Bray, having reached a very small size, refused to increase. We took them out on Sunday afternoons and did extended drill in the People's Park in the view of onlookers, but no one came forward to add to our numbers. I spoke to the men in the little place where we used to meet and asked them what we should do. They advised that we would go no further unless we drew upon new sections of the community, such as the shop assistants. To get such recruits would give us a greater respectability and encourage people to support us. I asked what they thought would be the most effective way of achieving this. They were unanimous in saying that we must have a public meeting. It should be on a Sunday afternoon, when all the people would be about, and the usual place to hold such meetings was at the top of the main street. I therefore decided to organize such a meeting.

It was about this time (the end of August, or beginning of September), that I had finally decided that my obedience to the order that I had received from the British Authorities was putting me and the movement generally in an absurdly anomalous position. I put the case before the Executive. We repudiated the right of the British Government to rule the country, we declared that we were the national armed force of

84

the Irish people, and yet that British Government had only to tell me that they would not allow me to enter Dublin, and I obediently accepted their order. The Executive agreed with my point of view. At the same time it appeared to me that having obeyed for so long if I were now just to cease to obey and, for instance go into Dublin, it might be thought that I was disobeying surreptitiously, hoping that it would not be observed. I therefore proposed that I should formally announce my intention to the British, and to this also the Executive agreed. On getting that assent, I wrote to Mr. Birrell who was then Chief Secretary, and told him that henceforth I intended to disregard the order. Having sent that letter I then allowed time for it to be received and noted, so it was probably a fortnight or ten days before I actually got on my bicycle and started off in the direction of Dublin. I went into Headquarters to make arrangement about the public meeting, for I felt that if it were to have the effect that we looked for, it must be made impressive. I arranged that Volunteers would come out to Bray from Dublin, and march to the meeting, so as to bring the people along with them, and that well-known leaders from Dublin should come and speak. Of course, O'Rahilly promptly promised to come, and to bring others. The arrangement was that I should preside.

On the Sunday arranged, a large body of men came out by train. They formed up in fours outside the station and headed by the leaders who had come, and by myself, we marched through the town, the men singing the marching songs that had become popular in the movement. A good crowd followed, to our great satisfaction. It meant that we should have an impressive meeting, quite independent of the number that we had brought from Dublin.

I remember that I felt that it must be made clear to the people that this was not just a meeting in favour of Home Rule such as they had been used to all their lives. I therefore set out in detail, in my speech, the powers that were necessary to possess if we were really to satisfy our national ambition. I named every Governmental power that I could think of that was not included in the Home Rule Bill that had been put upon the Statute Book and then suspended from operation. The O'Rahilly and the other speakers followed, and when the meeting was over we felt that it had been extremely successful, and that our doctrine had been put very clearly before the people although my own speech struck me as having been too restrained as compared with the others.

As we sat in my house that night, O'Rahilly assured me that he was convinced that it would bring about a great influx into the movement in that district. I felt quite sure of the same thing. In the crowd I had noted men whom I knew by sight who were listening and who certainly did not manifest any disapproval of the doctrine that was being put forward. We joked about the police who had attended the meeting in large numbers as they did at all such meetings.

The following days I had to give up exclusively to Volunteer work. In going round the country I had got a number of young men from different places in one wide area who were all willing to try to start the movement in their district. But all of them had insisted that it was impossible for them to go ahead unless we had the support of one man, whose name carried great weight in the whole area as a great patriotic leader. I had visited that man a number of times. He always received me with great cordiality, expressed the most extreme sentiments, constantly referred to the fact that he had been an I.R.B. man all his life, but at the same time put every conceivable obstacle in my way. I sized him up as one who had built up a reputation as a great patriot by preaching extreme sentiments when it was perfectly safe to do so, and who wanted to keep that position without attaching any risk to himself. I was quite satisfied that he wanted no Volunteers in his district as, if he remained aloof from them, he would have to come off his patriotic pedestal, while if he associated himself with them he might put himself in danger. For a long time a hidden tussle had been going on between us. My strength had been that he dared not come out openly against me, and his had been that he knew that unless he gave his support I could get nowhere in all that area. I had been trying to get the young men to stand up against his tacit opposition, and I had now got in touch with a man whose influence in that district was only second to that of my opponent, and I had forced this second man to promise to support me. During that week I was arranging to get together a meeting of all the leaders from various little districts in that one area, at which meeting my influential and secret opponent would be present as well as the other influential man who had given me to understand that he was prepared to assist me in every possible way.

The meeting came off one night that week. We assembled in a small hall in a village. The famous patriot seated himself at the head of the table as of right and I saw to it that my influential supporter would take the other end as a sort of vice-chairman.

I put forward the case that the young men present should start Volunteer companies in their respective districts. The Chairman opposed this by one means or another but was unable to make a convincing case. He argued that a better plan would be that the young men should start rifle clubs in their districts, and train themselves and their friends to shoot, and then when the moment came to strike a blow, they would be trained and ready. But he avoided as long as he could, putting forward any case against their being associated with the Volunteer movement. It looked as though I were going to win in spite of him. The other influential man remained rather quiet at his end of the table but I felt that he was ready to clinch the matter by coming to my side when the moment arrived. The young men showed every sign of supporting my case, and my opponent had not put forward any reason to stand against it. At last when he saw the way the meeting was moving he came out with a new argument. He knew every man present, and he was able to turn to them, and ask them did they want to lose their jobs through my madness. To one who was a teacher, and to others who had jobs that were in one way and another associated with the Government he was able to turn and deal

87

with their individual positions. I was asking them to come out and parade in the open in an organization whose declared aim was the overthrow of British power in Ireland. The British Government had power to take away their jobs, and then where would they be? I saw his words were telling in their effect. I invoked the vice-chairman, but he turned round and supported my opponent. Nothing that I could say could carry the meeting with me. I could only say that I gave the patriot a fortnight to get the rifle clubs going, with the men armed with proper rifles that would be useful in a Rising, and if at the end of that time, the clubs had not come into existence so armed I would go ahead in spite of the opposing patriot. They all agreed that that was a fair proposal from me. I was quite certain that there would be no clubs formed armed as I had demanded, but I also knew that those two influential men would do all in their power, and their power was much greater than mine, to make it impossible to start Volunteers in that district. The only success I had was that with regard to one district I did get the representative to agree that on the following Sunday (or it may have been the next Sunday after that) I should come down and drill the men.

That meeting had gone on until fairly late in the night. After it, I had to stay talking to all manner of people. It was in the early hours of the morning that I got on my bicycle to ride about twelve or thirteen miles home. The morning was well advanced before I got back to Bray.

I went to bed far from cheerful, and when I opened my eyes later that morning I looked out on the District Inspector and policemen beside the bed. I was told that I was under arrest, that I had better dress and go with them. They could not tell me the charge against me, but I would learn that in due course. When I was dressed I was taken first to the local police barracks, and from there to Mountjoy Gaol where I was duly lodged. But before going off I left word that Eimar O'Duffy should be sent to take my place in charge of the drill that I had arranged for the following Sunday (or the one after that). However I

88

heard later that when O'Duffy went he found that there were no young men in the village. My patriotic opponent had more resources than I was aware of. After leaving the meeting he had arranged that a football match should take place just at the time when the drill was due. The young men, of course, regarded it as unthinkable that they should miss a football match, for any reason short of an earthquake. And to attend a Volunteer drill fell far short of an earthquake in their minds. The result was that O'Duffy had his cycle ride for nothing.

Since the beginning of the war there had been a few arrests and imprisonments for activities arising out of the Volunteer movement, but at that time it was still far from being a usual occurrence. And in spite of my conversations with Blythe about his prison experience there seemed to be something of mystery and menace about what awaited me, but of course I had no intention of showing any but a cheerful exterior.

There are certain formalities attached to one's entrance as a prisoner, and the warders in charge of these were quite friendly and ready to make jokes about the position I found myself in, and to give me any information I asked about the prison régime. They told me that I would retain my own clothes and be allowed to have food sent in until such time as I was sentenced. They thought it particularly amusing that I should be a prisoner while neither they nor I knew what I was imprisoned for. They informed me that pending my trial I should have no work to do, that another prisoner would even see to the cleaning of my cell, and that I should take exercise in the yard with the 'remand prisoners'. Also that I should be allowed a visit a day, which must take place in the presence of a warder, but that I should be allowed to see my solicitor in private.

This seemed to me to be quite promising as it meant that the full conditions of prison life would only be gradually imposed; thus, I should have got used to most of the prison conditions before having to face prison diet.

I was taken to my cell, which was larger than I expected it to be and the door was locked upon me. The turning of the key in the lock gave me a feeling of isolation and impotence, but I was still able to smile to myself as I thought over some of the grotesque remarks of the warders I had been dealing with. Then the door was re-opened and a prisoner was brought to do some cleaning in the cell. While he was there the door was left open. The prisoner set about his work, and even called my attention to the way things were done, such as the cleaning of the tin or pewter wash bowl. Then he asked what I was in for, and I told him as well as I could. It was clear that ordinary good manners demanded that I should ask him about himself. But he was in such a hurry to tell that he hardly waited for me to frame the question. He was on remand for murder—the murder of his wife—but he was quite innocent. He entered into a long detailed account of all the events of the day of his wife's death. He had been away, it may have been at the war. He met his wife in Dublin and they had certain drinks. He gave an exact account of the public houses and the drinks consumed. They took the train to their own place in Kildare, and that night attended a wake. I think he gave an account of what they drank at the wake. His wife left for home at some hour of the night, but he stayed on and only left at a later hour. She was not at home when he arrived, and he went to bed. The next day her body was found in the canal. He was arrested for her murder, against all justice. He kept on going over the details, always repeating them in the same words. He seemed to tell the story so much by rote, that I was not convinced by it. I hoped it was true, and that in any case it would win him an acquittal, but I saw him as a man who had every prospect of being led out to execution. That thought seemed to take possession of my mind. Every time he came into the cell he went over again his account of that fatal day and night, and it seemed to me that it was all for the purpose of persuading himself that he would not have to face that fatal morning when the summons to execution would come. It seemed frivolous even to refer to what might be awaiting me in the way of imprisonment. At the back of his mind and of mine was the consciousness that every day might be bringing nearer the moment when the rope would be fastened about his neck. When I sat down to the meals that were brought in to me from outside the prison that thought would come back vividly, and I had to get up from my stool and pace up and down the cell, so that when the warder came in afterwards he would exclaim about the waste of money in sending good food in to me.

I had a daily visit from my wife. We sat with a wide counter between us, and a good humoured warder by my side. I got news of my friends and veiled hints that all was going on well outside. Then after a few days a warder came to me and told me that my solicitor had come to see me. I knew who he was. He was a member of the Executive. As our conversation would be in private I jumped up to hurry to the interview hoping to hear all that was known by the Executive itself.

The moment we were alone I began pouring out all the questions that had come into my mind while I was locked in the cell. But the solicitor wanted to talk about my own position, and the defence that was to be made. I told him that I had thought the matter out before my arrest and had decided that in such an event I would make no defence. He protested against that, and for the rest of the interview we argued that matter.

He came again the next day and the next, and always we debated the same question. He told me that the Executive would provide a good barrister and that the defence would have great propaganda value for our movement. Everybody else, including Sean MacDermott of the Executive, had been defended. I began to feel that the action (or rather inaction) that I proposed to take was thoroughly disapproved of, that it somehow ran quite against the policy of those I looked up to as leaders. Shut off from the outer world I felt that I had no means of judging things. It came to the point that when I heard the warders coming to my cell to summon me to an interview my heart sank inside me. On the one hand there was I insisting on taking a course that would commit me to a longer term of imprisonment and at the same time I would be condemned by

91

my friends as injuring the cause I was trying to serve. On the other hand, before my arrest, when I was able to view things clearly I had judged that the course I proposed was the only logical and dignified one for a man in my position. And in all those arguments with the solicitor I heard no news that made my previous decision invalid.

At last in desperation I said that if he could bring me a written message from the Executive, ordering me to act as he advised, I would do so, but otherwise I should follow my previous determination. At that he replied 'Of course, the Executive agrees that you are right in principle,' and he then went on to base his argument on the unbearableness of prison and my own interest in having my time there made as short as possible.

That relieved my mind immediately. I told him again that I had thought it all out before my arrest. That in my present circumstances I was unable to judge the matter, but provided that I was not incurring the disapproval of my superiors in the organization I should act as I had previously decided.

After that he did not come again, to my great relief. For I had come back from those interviews in a state of utter helpless depression, to be locked up in my cell with the feeling that I was alienating all my friends.

I had been in prison twelve days before I was told what charges were to be made against me. I think it was the D.I. who had arrested me who was brought to my cell with the charge sheet. It stated that I was accused of three offences—(i) making statements calculated to promote sedition; (ii) making statements calculated to discourage recruiting and (iii) disobeying a military order. At the same time I was informed that I would be tried at Bray on the following Saturday.

Walking around the ring at exercise I got to know a number of the remand prisoners. Naturally one opens conversations with a question as to what the man is in for. I was impressed by the fact that every man assured me that he was innocent, though most of the warders with whom I had conversations were far from convinced of their innocence. There was one tall man with a short trimmed beard, and a moustache that he obviously waxed each morning with a piece of yellow soap that was part of the equipment of every cell. I never spoke to him on the ring, as we were never next to each other. But from a warder I learned that he was charged with murder and a particularly brutal murder.

An elderly couple living in a tiny roadside cottage had amassed fairly considerable savings. At the outbreak of the war they had felt that everything might collapse and that even the banks were no longer safe. They had withdrawn their money and kept it concealed in their cottage. Then one morning they were both discovered dead with their heads battered in with a hammer, and the money gone. My fellow-prisoner was charged with their murder.

The only time I had conversation with him was on the morning of my trial. As one has no provision for shaving while in prison, it was customary for a man to be made 'respectable looking' for his trial by having another prisoner clip the growth from his face with a pair of scissors. It was this tall man with the waxed moustache who was chosen to improve my appearance. He did his job comparatively well, only twice did he nip my face and make it bleed. Even that was really due to the fact that he was more interested in talking to me than in his work. We did not discuss what he was in for, and he did not seem to have that tragic awareness of the fate that was possibly awaiting him that had marked the other man in a similar position. He gave me advice about the trial that I was going off to, and even other advice, such as—'Be very careful who you talk to here. There's a very mixed crowd in this place.'

That morning I felt like a boy when school is breaking up. After a fortnight in prison I was to be taken to Bray, to see the outer world and to see many of my friends who would be there for the trial, and I should be able to talk to them.

When I arrived at the Courthouse I found quite a number of them gathered there. We talked and joked until the magistrates entered. When they came to deal with my case I thought that

93

I, as the accused, had to sit in an elevated chair, but I was told that that was for witnesses, and I sat among my friends. The magistrates looked round for my solicitor, and when they found that there was none, they appeared to be annoyed.

The police official who prosecuted announced that there were three charges but that if I were found guilty on the first two they would not proceed with the third. The third was that I had disobeyed the military order, by entering a 'prohibited area'.

I had, of course, made up my mind that I would refute nothing that was charged against me. But when the police note-taker began reading out what purported to be my speech, I was horrified and indignant to find that I was represented as having treated the English language in my speech as the police-man himself did when he was not reading his notes. When he had finished the Chairman of the Bench asked if I had anything to say in reply to his evidence. I could only say that the report he had read was substantially, but not literally correct, and that I stood over it. Of course, there was applause in the court from all those who had come to give me support.

The magistrates retired. We knew quite well that they were certainly not going to bring in an acquittal. But all those whose good opinions I valued pressed round and assured me that the course I followed was the only right one. After all I had endured from those interviews with the solicitor those assurances were grateful to my soul.

When the magistrates returned they announced that my own attitude in court had simplified their work in bringing in a verdict. They found me guilty on the two charges brought forward and gave the maximum sentence on each charge, six months, both sentences to run concurrently. The prosecutor said that in view of that finding he would not go on with the third charge. One of the magistrates said that in view of my own attitude he had to agree with the finding but he demurred at the sentence as he thought that three months would be quite sufficient. However, I had expected six months and therefore was not downcast. I was at that moment exhilarated to know that my action was approved by my friends. I had taken the opportunity that I got there to tell Blythe and others about what I had suffered in my interviews with the solicitor. That exhilaration remained until I heard the familiar sound of the key turning in my cell lock. Then I was conscious of a flatness, and six months seemed to be a very long time.

Now I was no longer allowed to have my food sent in from outside. In effect that was the only change made by the fact that I was now a sentenced prisoner. For exercise I was changed from the remand ring to the sentenced ring, but that made no difference. I now had work to do but it was only sewing bags in my cell, and if there was any fixed amount to be done, it was such that I could do it and still have all the time I wanted for walking up and down. I still wore my own clothes. I now had to clean up the cell and the few utensils that it contained. Now I was only allowed one letter and one visit a month, but to my surprise I found that there was a visit due immediately after sentence.

I tried to force myself to eat the food that I was given. But the shell cocoa without milk or sugar I found unpalatable. The bread which was made in the prison had a sour smell and tasted of sour yeast. I sipped the cocoa and could not continue, I tore off a small piece of bread and nibbled it, but there again I could not continue. I knew that I was difficult about food, and wanted to overcome that as soon as possible, but that first evening, the next day and the next, of all the food brought in I could take nothing but the milk which figured in the diet. Two warders commented on the fact that I was not eating. When they had taken the food away they would come and ask if I were hunger striking. I hastily contradicted that idea, and assured them that I would eat in due time but I would have to get very hungry first. The rumour spreading round that I was on hunger strike worried me. I had to prevent it from being accepted. I had always been quite convinced that hunger striking was morally indefensible, and I did not want my name associated with such a course. Also I had made up my mind to settle down to the food there—I still had in mind that when the condition of the Rising came about I must be able to eat anything that the other men could eat—and I did not want to have the reputation of starting a hunger strike and then abandoning it. Also to hunger strike seemed to me completely illogical and undignified. I had known quite well that the British power in Ireland was established and that it could put us in prison if we stood out against it. It seemed ridiculous to set out to overthrow that power, and then to kick at the consequences as they affected oneself. To hunger strike seemed to me to suggest that I was surprised and horrified at what my action had brought on me, whereas I had acted with my eyes open. But to the warders who were constantly coming to my cell it seemed clear that a prisoner either ate his food, or did not because he was hunger striking and for no other reason. Of course, as a matter of fact, I was taking all the milk that I received.

I certainly felt hungry, but in spite of that I still found it impossible to overcome my repugnance when Tuesday arrived. Then as I walked up and down my cell I felt something in my overcoat. I examined it and found that it was a bar of chocolate that had slipped down through the pocket, and had not been noticed by the warders who searched my clothes. I kept it until the bread was brought in. Then I ate the bread with the chocolate which concealed the sour taste. When the warder came to collect the meal utensils, I pointed out to him that I had eaten the bread. That convinced him that I was not hunger striking, and thereafter by slow degrees I got used to the cocoa and other items of diet, though right until the end there were some things that I could not eat, such as the slab of suet pudding that formed the chief meal on Sundays. I looked on this dietary triumph as a great step for preparing myself for the Rising that was to come.

There was the question as to whether the Rising might not be started while I was still in prison. I had raised this with O'Rahilly when I saw him at my trial. He said that of course one of the first acts would be to release any of our men that might be in prison. I had accepted that assurance, but nevertheless I was always trying to get any news I could from the warders that might show if there were signs of our people taking action.

For the first fortnight I only went out of my cell to take exercise in the yard. I noticed from the whispered conversations that I had with other prisoners that that confinement to the cell was regarded as a great hardship. They all took opportunity to assure me that after a couple of weeks I should be allowed to work outside. I could not see why they looked upon my present condition as hard, or why they thought that it would be such a great improvement when it was changed in that respect.

It was while I was still spending twenty-two hours a day in my cell that a warder told me that the man who had cleaned my cell had been tried for the murder of his wife and found guilty. The exercise yard for condemned prisoners was just under my window, and I could hear the unfortunate man walking round there every day at the time when the rest of us were having our midday meal. The horror of his position weighed down on me. I used to picture to myself his thoughts either walking round there or in his cell. When I was finally told that he had been reprieved and his sentence commuted to one for life, it brought me the relief that it probably brought to him. At least I suppose that it did bring him relief, though indeed the prospect of spending the next twenty years in prison could hardly bring him much joy once he faced up to it.

At the end of a fortnight I was taken out to the woodyard and put in a little shed to sit on a stump of wood and break stones. I found this a not unpleasant way of passing the time in prison. There seemed to be no particular amount of stones that had to be broken, but one had no desire to shirk the work as it was mechanical and rather soothing. Later on I was promoted to chopping blocks of wood into little sticks for kindling fires, and still later to making those sticks into bundles. I developed a sort of enthusiasm for this latter work. One pressed the sticks

97

together in a vice, tied a rosined string about them, released the vice and piled the little bundles one on top of the other. I felt a pride in my work as I watched the pile of bundles growing. I felt like an athlete when he learns that he has broken the record. But some of the other prisoners viewed it with disapproval. They seemed to think that it was against some trade union rule. As for me, it seemed to me that as I had to spend so many hours a day in the little shed and to spend so many days and weeks in the prison I might just as well spend the time working (it was not laborious) as in doing nothing, or trying to do the minimum.

At exercise and in the woodyard I got to know a number of prisoners. Most of them seemed to be habituals. A new prisoner would arrive and instead of having to be told the routine, he would assume a most superior air and indicate that he knew much more about it than the warders. As indeed he might for in many cases prisoners had spent more time in and out of the prison than the warders had.

Making bundles of wood in the next little shed to mine in the woodyard was a 'B' class prisoner, that is to say a man who had been sentenced to imprisonment in the second division. As such he was to be treated differently from ordinary third division prisoners, of which I was one. To be in the second class indicated a superior status, but apart from that it had little advantage except that such a prisoner received from the beginning 'D' diet which we others had a right to only after we had been in prison for some months.

Although my own status was officially identical with that of the ordinary prisoners, the prison authorities apparently regarded me as somewhat different. The second division prisoner always had to be at the end of the line of prisoners when we marched to and from the woodyard. I was last but one, and as I have said I worked next to him. He told me all about his case. He had been in the Paymaster's Office in Dublin, and held a sergeant's rank. He dealt with marriage allowances for soldiers

98

Desmond Fitzgerald (*c.* 1922).

(*Photo: Topical Press Agency.*)

Desmond Fitzgerald at a Celtic Congress in the early '20's.

and had worked out some plan whereby he issued a warrant for a marriage allowance, cashed it himself in a post office and when the voucher from the post office came into the paymaster's office, it came to him and he was able to destroy it. In this way he was able to give himself a considerable amount of money and it had seemed that he would be able to continue to do so indefinitely. But unfortunately for him he had to take his annual leave. He went off to England and had a great holiday with either his own motor car or his own motor bicycle. But when he arrived back at Kingstown there were men waiting for him with a charge of embezzlement. As we worked away making our bundles he explained to me that his method had been so perfect that as long as he was on the spot no one could have detected the fraud. The only thing he had overlooked was the fact that his absence made discovery inevitable. He was very conscious of his superior status as a prisoner, and looked down with great scorn on the ordinary third division men. But he assured me that he recognized me as a man of education. His misfortune had not destroyed his natural cheeriness or his sense of humour.

Occasionally warders would come and stand by my shed and have a whispered conversation with me, when it was certain that the Governor would not be making his visit. One warder in particular always took his post there and pointed out to me what a damn fool I was to be in the position I then was. Other warders told me a version of his history. According to them he had been a higher grade warder, but feeling himself very knowledgeable was always arguing with everybody he met. He had read as a boy about the campaign of James II in Ireland and his great topic was that if at that time, when a king and army were fighting in Ireland supported by the Irish and even then they were beaten, it was only madness for anyone to expect that in the less favourable position that had existed ever since and must continue to exist, the Irish people could hope for any kind of freedom from English overlordship.

On one occasion an argument on this point had developed in

99

a public house between the warder and another man which culminated in a fight. The other man was a policeman in plain clothes. The warder was reduced in rank as a result. To have held a higher position and to be reduced to a lower in the same service put the man in an impossible position. Those who had been beneath him, and whom he had lorded it over, took every opportunity to humiliate him. In desperation he had thought that if he became a Protestant he would commend himself to those in authority and be restored to his previous rank. He had done so and waited patiently for the anticipated mark of appreciation, but it never came. In the end when he found that nothing was coming of his action, he came back to the Church. Whether the version that the other warders told me was exactly true, I do not know, but whatever the truth was, they regarded him with a devastating contempt.

Another warder who came and stood by my shed seemed to be always in a state of wild excitement. This was explained as being due to the fact that at some time a boiler had exploded and he had been blown up with it. In a breathless and irascible way he would ask me to explain various things that he read in the papers. At that time, apparently there were references to the Ruthenians and he asked me to tell him all about the Ruthenians. I began to tell what I knew, but he burst in saying that he wanted to know were they Catholics or what were they. I explained that they were Uniates, that they acknowledged the supremacy of the Pope, but belonged to a different rite from the Latin.

'But what the Hell does that mean,' said he, 'either they are Catholics or they aren't.'

'They are,' said I, 'but there are certain differences between us, for instance their priests can marry.'

'If their priests marry,' said he, 'then it's damn certain that they aren't Catholics.'

I thought to make the matter clear by telling him that when the Eucharistic Congress was held in London, priests of the Eastern Uniate Church who were allowed to marry, had not only been there but that the Cardinal had arranged that they should say Mass according to the Eastern Rite in Westminster Cathedral. I began laboriously enough, saying—'Now I was in London . . .' but he allowed me to get no further. He burst in—'I don't care if you was. I don't care if you was in Rome, inside in the Pope's stomach.' Then he hurried away.

The second division man in his shed next door who had listened to the conversation, leaned out and said—'That clinched the argument, didn't it?'

There were also some German prisoners in the woodyard. They came there having been sentenced for trying to escape from the Internment Camp. One of them I knew about, as another of our men who had been in Mountjoy before me and had been released before I was arrested had known him there. This prisoner was a Bavarian, and he lived up to the reputation of his people, by always being gay. This made him popular with everyone, and particularly with the warders. As he had probably been there the longest, he had the most exalted jobs. For one part of the time he was dipping the bundles of wood in the boiling rosin and in the evening he came round with a barrow to collect the bundles that we had made. In that way we got little talks together and became good friends. But before my time was half over his time was up. We said good-bye, and I felt that the woodyard would not be the same after he had gone.

But of these German prisoners, the one I got to know best was Hans Christian Deichmann. He came from Schleswig Holstein. His grandfather had been born before the Germans became masters there, and probably never spoke German. Hans felt himself to be completely German, but he also spoke Danish as a Dane. He was a sailor, and loving his craft of the sea had always by choice sailed in German sailing ships. He had been shipwrecked a number of times. His ship had left America before war was declared. But they had been told of the war by another ship that passed them in mid-ocean. When the ship came near the Irish coast a British war vessel had taken them into tow, and brought them to Cork Harbour. From there Hans and his shipmates had been taken to the Camp at Templemore and later they were transferred to Oldcastle.

His mind was possessed of the idea that at all costs he must fight for his country. Even if he were to be killed in a short time he wanted to have participated in the war. He made up his mind to try to get back to Germany. He made his plans without speaking a word of them to anybody. He had fifteen shillings in his pocket when one night he worked his way through the barbed wire. He walked on all night and concealed himself during the day. He was making his way to Limerick, hoping to get on to any Danish ship that might be there. He had heard that begging was illegal in Ireland, so for food he called at farmhouses and asked to buy it. But in all his long walk no farmer had taken a penny of his money. On one occasion he felt that he wanted what he called a 'blow-out' with bread and jam, and he ventured into a village and spent one and sixpence. That was the only money he parted with on his journey. At another time on a glorious day he was beside a lake. He had an idea that it was on the borders of King's County and Westmeath. He took off his clothes and bathed and absorbed the beauty of the lake scene. Feeling hungry later on he went to a farmhouse that stood well off the road. The farmer received him well and asked him who he was. He told the story that he had decided on before he left the camp, that he was a Danish sailor making his way to his ship. The farmer looked at him and said—'I'll tell you who you are. You are Hans Deichmann and you escaped from the camp at Oldcastle.' Hans thought all was lost. But the farmer reassured him.

'You're with friends here,' he said. 'Why not stay with us until the war is over. We can keep you concealed all right and you'll be quite comfortable here.'

The farmer's daughter joined with her father.

'It was very tempting,' said Hans. 'They were lovely Irish people. I should have liked to stay with them. But I told the farmer that I had escaped because I wanted to fight for my country. And then he said he wouldn't try to keep me. But he told me to come in and have a good dinner with them. They gave me a wonderful meal. And then the daughter filled my pockets with food and apples. I wish I knew where that place was. I should like to see them again when the war is over, and tell them thanks.'

In all he was three weeks walking from Oldcastle to Limerick. When he got there he saw a Danish vessel and went aboard. He told the Captain the truth about himself and the Captain was quite willing to take him, but he said that his ship had to call at a number of English ports before it went back to Denmark and Hans might easily be spotted and taken off to prison. But the Captain pointed out another Danish ship that would be going straight back to Denmark, and advised him to try that one.

He did so, but on this occasion he had not liked to tell the truth, and told the story about being a Danish sailor which was convincing as he spoke Danish as a Dane. This Captain also agreed to take him, and all was going well until just as the ship was leaving. Then the police decided to come aboard to see that all was well. They asked to see papers, and when it came to Hans' turn he could produce none. They immediately became suspicious, especially when the Captain could say so little about him. When the police decided to take Hans off the ship, he told the truth to the Captain in Danish so that the police could not understand. The Captain said—'Why didn't you tell me that. I could easily have hidden you aboard and they would never have found you.' But it was too late then. Hans was identified as the escaped prisoner, brought to trial and he had been sentenced to six months just ten days before I was. So we were to spend nearly our whole time in Mountjoy together. He would leave just ten days before my time would be up.

Hans had a passion for that suet pudding that I found un-eatable. He said that he had always liked going aboard an English ship because it formed part of the men's diet there. I always gave him my share which represented no sacrifice whatever on my part, but he always received it with great joy. On Christmas Day, he came to me with great joy with his piece of plum pudding, which was the special treat to celebrate that day. He said that he knew that I liked sweet things and had saved it for me.

Some time after I had settled in Mountjoy two other Germans came in. They also were sentenced for escaping from Oldcastle. But they had made more elaborate plans than Hans and in spite of that were caught much more quickly. They had been allowed to go out in the village to make purchases for the prisoners. In that way they were able to make friends with some of the people, and arranged to get clothes as clergymen in which to escape. But having got away they did not exercise Hans' caution. One of them thought that he spoke English so well that no one would know that he was a foreigner. As a matter of fact one would know immediately that he only spoke English with difficulty. But he felt so confident that instead of avoiding people he was ready to go up and speak to everyone he passed on the road. The result was that within a couple of days they were arrested.

And later on two others came. One was named Pockmeyer. They had also escaped through the barbed wire and were caught fairly quickly. But by the time that they were brought to trial the punishment was increased and they were sentenced to twelve months. I heard afterwards that when they were released poor Pockmeyer again tried to escape from Oldcastle but while he was entangled in the barbed wire the sentry saw him and fired and he was killed.

One Saturday night I heard a great commotion as a prisoner was brought in and a warder said—'That's another of your kind arrived.' I thought that it must be a Volunteer. But when I pressed for more information, it appeared that the new man had been running a campaign against cinema films that he thought objectionable. He had gone to a picture house and thrown a bottle of ink at the screen and then gone to the front of the screen and made a speech. He was arrested and fined five shillings for destroying the screen, or alternatively sentenced to three days' imprisonment. He had been escorted to Mountjoy by a procession of his admirers. I thought that he might have news, and the next day I got next to him on the exercise ring. I told him who I was and asked if he had any news of the Volunteers. He indicated that the leaders of the movement gave him all their confidence, but I could not find that he knew anything to tell me. He kept on assuring me that the country had put a halo round my head and worshipped me with profound reverence. Unfortunately, this was not very convincing as he seemed also to be determined that an even greater reverence should be paid to him for what he had done. The three days' sentence meant that having come in on Saturday night he would be released as soon as cell doors were opened on Monday, so there was no further opportunity to talk with him.

But there were other prisoners who came in while I was there who were directly or indirectly associated with the Volunteers. One man came to the woodyard, sentenced, I think, to a month. The charge against him was some Volunteer activity. It was a great joy to both of us, I think, when we got the chance to talk.

Then there were two young men who were members of the body called the Citizen Army, which was controlled from Liberty Hall, the Labour headquarters. They were actually charged with stealing copper from the Railway works, but they had been taking the copper to make munitions for their Volunteer Organization. One was named Conroy. I do not remember the name of the other man, though I met them both afterwards.

I saw another man whom I had known in the movement before I came to prison. That was Alec McCabe. He was on remand charged with the possession of explosives. My only chance to get a word with him was as he passed my cell door when it was open. Of course he took his exercise with the remand prisoners, and did not come near the woodyard. He was tried by a jury and found innocent. I am not at all certain that a lawyer would agree that the finding was in accord with the evidence. But it meant that he did not appear again in Mount-joy after he went to trial.

CHAPTER SEVEN

Preparations for the Rising

During my earlier days in Mountjoy I had heard prisoners saying that they were due for release in a fortnight, in a week or in a few days, and I had thought that it must be wonderful for them. But as my own time was drawing to an end I found that my days were just the same. Each twenty-four hours were just the same if one were getting out in a week or in six months. Each evening I could count that I was a day nearer to release, but I was still a prisoner. Certainly one was saved that blank prospect that must oppress the mind of a man who knows that he must remain in prison for years ahead. But release has no real meaning until it is a fact. Or only very little meaning.

After six months in prison I found it impossible to sleep on the night before release, though I was very anxious to do so, in order to bring the wonderful moment nearer. I could assure myself that when morning came I should be free again, but I still had to wait for the morning to come, that morning of March 31, 1916 that had been fixed in my mind ever since the moment I was sentenced. The hours of the night seemed interminable, but they did come to an end. The warders realized that every minute mattered to me, and as soon as the cells were opened I was taken to the reception room which was also the discharge room. I was allowed to shave. The things that had been taken when I was searched on coming in were brought together with some other things that had been sent in on the assumption that I should be allowed to have them. I remember that the register showed that a box of collars had come for me, whereas only one collar was forthcoming. The warder was flurried about this as it indicated that some purloining had taken place, but I told him not to worry about that. A few collars were of no importance to me just then. There were also some letters that had come without my being told of them. One of these was from a group of English poet friends who sent little booklets of translations they had made from the Latin and Greek poets. In their letter they said that they sent them as they thought that even in prison it would please me to know that the War had not completely killed poetry in England. I had not been allowed to know that they had sent the booklets or the letter until now when I was leaving prison, but I did rejoice to know that I had not lost the friendship of those poets, for I had thought that the news that I was sentenced as an enemy of England during that time of war fever might have ended that old friendship.

I had decided in my own mind that I should like a holiday when I came out, and that everybody would agree to that as they all seemed to look upon imprisonment as a much greater ordeal than it really was. In any case after that long isolation I would require some time to get back into things again. But that pleasant prospect did not live for long. When I came out through the outer gate O'Rahilly and my wife were there with his car, and as soon as our first greetings were over, I turned to him and said:

'Well, how's the Rising getting on? When is it coming off.'

'It may come off this week-end', he replied. 'Certainly things are moving fast, and there are some signs that it may start tomorrow or the day after.'

That did away with any prospect of a leisurely holiday. But we said no more about it then. My question had interrupted questions of theirs about the prison. O'Rahilly pointed out that he had brought some oranges in the car thinking that I might like to start on them immediately after the long course of prison diet. I did start on an orange, but there was so much to be said that I had not finished it before we arrived at the house.

Everything seemed wonderful to me. It was as though I saw the world with a fresh vision after being shut away from it for what seemed to me to be such a long time. And the company of one's own intimates was such a change from that of prisoners and warders. Even the streets which were almost deserted and very cold at that hour of a March morning, seemed beautiful. And even more so when we entered the house was the warmth and sight of the fire, and even the smell of the bacon that was being brought in for breakfast. I had to tell about my prison experiences, and when I began I found that it was one long series of amusing occurrences. I had to admit, after we had been talking for a long time that prison life contained much that was reminiscent of a really entertaining evening at a Music Hall.

Among the many items of news that they had to tell me was that Blythe and Liam Mellowes had received an order telling them that they must leave Ireland, and that at the same time they had been arrested. They were now in Arbour Hill Military Prison waiting to be transported to England. Each of them had been told the names of two or three places in England and he could choose from them which one he wished to be sent to. After being taken there he must report his arrival to the local police, must not leave the district, and must report himself to the police station every few days. I was told also that while in Arbour Hill they were allowed a visit every day, and that as I would naturally want to see Blythe, it had been arranged that I should take that day's visit.

I said that I knew Blythe well enough to know that he would not actively obey any instruction he got from the British. I could not see him choosing the place they wanted to transport him to, and reporting regularly to the police.

O'Rahilly then told me that the solicitor member of the Executive who had made my early days in prison memorable had been sent in to see Blythe as his legal advisor to tell him that he was to obey every order that the British gave him, as arrangements would be made to get him back surreptitiously for the Rising. That information was an item of evidence that the Rising was now recognized as fairly imminent. And O'Rahilly then detailed certain other symptoms that suggested that its imminence was closer still. O'Rahilly also warned me (quite unnecessarily) to make no reference to those instructions when I saw Blythe that day, as, of course, at my visit an official of the prison would be present.

There was nothing surprising in the fact that O'Rahilly, though a member of the Volunteer Executive and an office holder, should be in the dark as to what decisions if any were made about the Rising. Long before I was arrested it had been the position that these matters were really being decided by a smaller group within the Executive itself. This smaller group was understood to consist of those who were also on the controlling board of the I.R.B. Those who were not made their confidants observed closely all statements, decisions and actions, to deduce from them whether or not the moment was near at hand.

At an earlier stage we had assumed that the factor that would be the decisive element would be the position in the Great War. We had taken it for granted that we should be co-operating with a great power whose forces and equipment would be brought to Ireland. Consequently we had watched the War to see if it would develop in such a way that the Germans would be able to establish military contact with us. That meant that they should achieve such a position on the seas that their ships would be able to come safely to points on the Irish coast where bodies of troops and appropriate equipment could be landed.

O'Rahilly's opinion that the moment was so near (which he supported by much evidence that made it appear to be very probably correct), gave a new aspect to the situation. According to our previous views the two things that would decide that the moment was at hand were either that the Germans had such success on the Western Front, and more particularly on the sea, that the difficulties to their lending substantial aid would have disappeared, or that there was evidence that the end of the War was at hand. The news at the time gave no indication that either of these two conditions were about to be fulfilled. And yet the general demeanour of all the knowledgeable people I met that day, and the various items of news and gossip that I got from them, confirmed the deductions that O'Rahilly had made.

It was an exciting, but not a cheering prospect. I knew something of the strength, or rather the weakness of the Volunteers as compared with the resources of those they were to be pitted against. The War had acquired an appearance of semi-permanency which meant that even wild optimism could hardly hope that we should still be in the field when the time of general peace would come. And not being in the field meant that we should have been wiped out. The amount of force that would be required to deal with us would hardly be missed from the battlefields of Europe where men were massed in their millions with hitherto unheard of masses of warlike machinery.

When I left O'Rahilly's there were just two things that I had to attend to, and apart from those I knew that for the remainder of the day I should be meeting various people, and I tried to hope that from one or other of them I should get some information that would shed a more cheerful light on the position.

Of the two things I had to attend to one was to visit Blythe in Arbour Hill Prison, and the other was to find somebody who was, or who could be represented to be, a public man to preside at a public meeting that was to be held. This meeting was to 'protest against the action of the British Government in forcibly deporting out of Ireland Irishmen who were guilty of no crime but serving Ireland'. In other words it was to protest against the action taken against Blythe and Mellowes. It had been thought that I, having just come out of prison would be an appropriate chairman for that occasion. But I felt that I should have to have some time to get used to the outer world of men before I could face a crowd and make myself articulate to them.

Consequently I had to save myself by getting some other person to take my place. I actually got a man who was well-known in the Trades Union Movement to agree to take the chair.

Then I went on to see Blythe. A sergeant sat with us during the interview. He told me that he had been invited to choose between two places in England to be sent to. One of them was Abingdon. I asked which he would choose and he said that he certainly was not going to choose any. This surprised me in view of my having heard that instructions had been sent into him to obey every order he got from the British. I came back to the subject and talked around it as well as I could in view of the presence of the sergeant. I asked had his solicitor been in to see him, and he said he had. And added very significantly, 'the same one that went to see you and made you miserable until you put him in his place'. It was quite evident to me that he had not received his instructions.

After I left him I saw O'Rahilly and told him that Blythe did not know that he was to obey all the commands of the British authorities. O'Rahilly was puzzled at this, and said that perhaps the solicitor had decided only to give the order at a later visit.

As a matter of fact, as I learned afterwards, what had happened was, that when the solicitor made his visit, Blythe had well in mind what I had suffered. And when he had opened the conversation by saying 'Of course you will choose a place to be sent to,' it had seemed to Blythe that he was taking just the same line as he had taken with me, and so he answered 'Of course I shall do no such thing.' He must have said this in such a truculent way that the solicitor cleared away from that subject and did not refer to it again. The result was that Blythe got no instructions as to the course he was to follow, and took the line that he and I had agreed the previous year was the only one compatible with dignity.

When I left him I went back to the Volunteer Offices in Dawson Street, and spent the rest of the day there, for apart from those who worked in the offices there was a constant coming and going of people whom I knew, and as I said 'Goodbye' to one I had to say 'Hullo' to another. Those who were not in the innermost secrets would whisper to me that things were moving very rapidly. 'It can't be long now.' Tommy MacDonagh came in, all smiles as usual, and with plenty of talk. Everything was going splendidly. The movement was growing, enthusiasm was not wanting. Germany was bound to win the War, and we were going towards victory. But he did not tell me if the date of the Rising was fixed and when it was to be. There were plenty of grounds for his not doing so. For one thing it was important that the secret should be known by the fewest possible number, and for another there was a constant coming and going of people that made any very private conversation difficult. Pearse came in and talked with that gravity that he always showed and from him also I learned nothing definite. Eamonn Ceannt, who also presumably had a good idea of what was to happen, gave no information. The Secretary of the Volunteers [Bulmer Hobson] was not in the confidence of the knowledgeable men, and he was frankly critical. 'They are determined to go ahead,' he said, 'and nothing will stop them. They will ruin the whole movement. Germany is going to win, and we should hold our hand. If we did that everything would be certain. But they are mad.'

I don't know how many people I talked to that afternoon, but summing up what I had heard from those who knew much and from those who knew less I was quite convinced that the Rising was coming soon irrespective of what was happening in the War.

The 'Protest' meeting was successful. A big crowd gathered to which fact we gave more significance than it really deserved, as the meeting was held in an open space in the centre of Dublin where there are always plenty of people who are ready to gather into any crowd. But Tommy MacDonagh who was the last speaker, excelled even his natural eloquence, and just at the end of his speech he had a brilliant idea. Everybody had stated

113

as a general principle that the way to show our indignation at the action of the British Government was to rally to the Volunteers. But Tommy seized the occasion to call upon those present to line up there and then, to enrol as Volunteers and to have their first drill on the spot. Of course only a minority of those present responded by stepping into the ranks, but that minority was itself quite a large number. They were put through preliminary drill and then formed into a procession to march. This was so successful that it was decided to have such protest meetings every night for a week in different parts of Dublin, and to make them recruiting meetings at the same time. As far as I remember Tommy MacDonagh came to all of them. His unfailing eloquence was sure to be a great asset. It was at the Donnybrook meeting that week that I first met Mr. De Valera, who was an officer in that area.

The custom of our friends coming out to us in Bray had continued while I was in Prison, and during that time the Secretary of the Volunteers and his fiancée had joined the band of regular visitors. I now found that they were all critical, and even bitterly critical of those of the inner circle. Having been out of touch with things for so long I could do little more than ask questions. Those who were members of the Executive, and even the others of us, were of course in a completely false position. The Executive members shared the joint responsibility for the organization, and they were well aware that they were not being consulted in the all important matter that might commit those they were responsible for to immediate death. They were not even being made aware of what was to decide the moment for action. But they had good reason to believe that that was being fixed, or had already been fixed without regard to what developments might be taking place in the War. I could but sympathize with those friends whom I had known for long, and knew to be utterly sincere, and who were yet treated as though they were not to be trusted. Indeed on one or two occasions I was made quite indignant when I was speaking to members of that inner circle to see that they waived aside

Arthur Griffith and Desmond Fitzgerald, 1921.

(Photo: Radio Times Hulton Picture Library.)

(Photo: Independent Newspapers Limited.)
The General Post Office, Dublin, after the Easter rising.

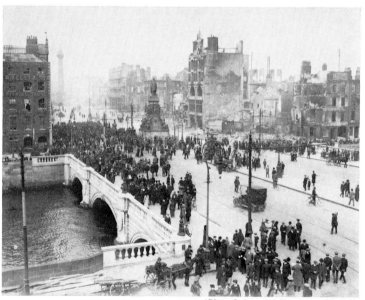

(Photo: Independent Newspapers Limited.)
O'Connell Street, Dublin, at the time of the 1916 rising.

all mention of those men in whose integrity I had complete confidence.

On the other hand I could also see that it was all important that there should be no leakage of information about the plans for the Rising, and that therefore they should be made known only to those who must necessarily be told. But at the same time I was told, under pledge of absolute secrecy that arrangements had been made for a shipment of arms from Germany. My wife knew that there was some secret information conveyed to me but I felt bound not even to let her know what it was. And when I was with men who were in positions of much greater responsibility than mine and heard them guessing as to what was being arranged by their colleagues, I felt that it was a kind of treachery on my part to know what was concealed from them.

On the Sunday night, a little more than a week after my release there was a concert in a hall in Parnell Square. The temper of the audience required that the songs should be of a propagandist nature and that there should be speeches. I was sitting with the Secretary of the Organization. Speeches were made extolling our movement and glorifying an armed Rising, per se. Somebody came down from the platform to urge that I should make a speech. But I refused to do so because it seemed perfectly clear that one who had been away from things as long as I had could have nothing of value to say to those who had been in continual touch with the course of events, and consequently it seemed that I was selected merely to invite applause for having suffered imprisonment. I may have suggested in refusing that it would be more appropriate that my neighbour should speak, seeing that he was a member of the Executive and General Secretary. In any case as he was present while I was being urged to speak, there was no valid reason for not inviting him. He immediately accepted, and made a speech that would probably have been unexceptional were it not that we were on the eve of the Rising. To the best of my memory he stressed the fact that in making a decision to take such action one was bound to see to it that the right moment was chosen and that it should not be hurried when postponement might give greater prospect of a successful issue.

One could feel that he was treading on dangerous ground. There was a certain breathlessness in the Hall. One could see glances passing between those who were probably aware of what decisions had already been taken. When it was all over there were groups talking earnestly together, some denouncing him and others praising his speech.

On the following days that speech was a general subject of conversation. Opinions differed from those who thought that it was a timely word of caution, to those who thought that it was black treachery. It was quite clear that those who knew most about the plans regarded it as disastrous.

I spent all the time I could in the Volunteer Offices, because among other jobs that I had been told to see to was the conversion of a big store of shot-gun cartridges into buckshot cartridges which I was told had to be completed as soon as possible. There were a number working at this, and when I was there supervising and lending a hand with the work, people would constantly come in to talk about the way the situation was developing, and those who were not in the confidence of the inner circle would bring in items of news that they thought indicated the imminence of the revolt.

It was O'Rahilly who had asked me to look after the conversion of the cartridges to buckshot and he was constantly coming to the room where the work was taking place. Indeed, during that period we were together as much as possible. He was in an impossible position, and there was hardly anybody to whom he could talk with absolute freedom. Many people came to him, assuming that occupying the position he did he must be aware of all the secret arrangements. To tell them that that was not the case was to convey to their minds that there was a split at headquarters and would be disloyal. It would also suggest that he was not trusted, with the implications that that

116

contained. He was uneasy in his mind, with the moral certainty that decisions had been made that were kept from him because they were such that he could not approve of, and yet the very position he held presented him as agreeing either explicitly or passively to young men being led to their death according to plans that he was not aware of and concerning which he was kept in darkness because in all probability his judgment would lead him to oppose them.

Meanwhile, Blythe had been duly deported to England, to Abingdon, and on the Sunday after the Concert in Parnell Square I received word from him that having arrived there and not having obeyed the order to report himself to the police he had been arrested and lodged in the lock-up, and was now due to be tried by a local branch of magistrates charged with disobeying that order. This confirmed what I had suspected when I visited him in Arbour Hill, that the message that was sent in to him had not been conveyed.

My wife and I immediately hurried in to Dublin and went to the Secretary of the Volunteers, who was an intimate friend of Blythe. He was gravely disturbed by this news but asked what could be done. I said that a messenger must be sent over immediately to see Blythe, to get a defence for him, and to arrange for his being got back to Ireland as soon as possible after he was released. The Secretary asked where could we get a messenger able to go immediately. My wife offered. It was then arranged that she should catch the boat that evening, go to London, and there get a friendly solicitor to look after the defence, and that if Blythe were not sentenced it should be arranged that he should be most obedient to his orders for a few days until the police ceased to be watchful, that during that time he should make a habit of going for walks, extending those walks from day to day, and that when the police were lulled into unsuspicion, a motor should pick him up on the road, and bring him to a port where arrangements should be made for him to get on a boat that would bring him to Ireland where he could go into hiding until the Rising took place, if it were

117

to take place. My wife hurried off to catch the boat, I having arranged a code with her so that if there were any special developments while she was away I should be able to warn her of them.

The general atmosphere of excitement had been growing in the Volunteer office and in Volunteer circles ever since I had come out of prison. And now it became more than ever apparent that the general 'tempo' was increasing. This seemed to reach its climax on the following Wednesday.

On that day I found when I arrived that what seemed to be an enormous amount of surgical dressings were brought into one of the offices, and members of the women's organization were called in to arrange for the making of field dressings and this work was treated as of immediate urgency. Members of the inner circle came in and out, and when there they retired into a room to hold secret conferences. Bundles of a leaflet which purported to be a secret order of the British that had been decoded were brought in and were being sent through the country for distribution. In the evening Mr. Pearse came in to have a talk with me, about what views I had formed moving about in Kerry and Wicklow as to the reactions of the Volunteers to active service. I remember that during that conversation I said that of course I did not know when the Rising was to take place but that from many symptoms that I had noted I felt that it was drawing near. He nodded his head gravely without saying whether that was a correct surmise, but at the same time seeming to indicate that it was a very natural surmise. I remember also that I said that from my experience I was satisfied that Volunteer companies that were only newly formed, say those that had not been more than six months in existence, would not have reached the point of thinking that they would really be called upon to take up arms. He considered that for a while and then said that I was certainly right in that. I then said that I also thought that companies that were isolated, that is to say companies in places where there were no other Volunteers in the neighbouring districts, should also be

118

regarded as not likely to take part in the Rising, and again he considered that for some moments, and said that I was probably right. I did not go so far as to ask directly when the Rising was to take place and neither did he volunteer that information, but it was quite clear that he intended me to know that not much time now remained. And, as though he thought that I might expect him to tell me all that was to be told, he went on to hint rather than to say that he and his colleagues had complete confidence in me, but in doing so it seemed to me that he was implying that I was rather unfortunate in my associates. I therefore took care to bring in the names of some of my friends and to make it clear that I knew that no concern for their own safety entered into their thoughts. To that he said nothing.

That conversation, coming after the general atmosphere of tension that had marked the day, satisfied me that I should now make use of the code that I had arranged with my wife. I therefore sent her a note that things were moving so rapidly that I thought that she should catch the boat on Saturday night or she might be too late for the Rising.

At the same time, I am not at all certain that it was not the alleged decoded message that operated most in my mind. I was certainly not entirely convinced that this was not made by our own people. But if it were indeed a true copy of instructions sent out by the British, then it did indicate that the British were about to take action, and if they did it meant that the Rising would be precipitated. Whereas if, as I thought possible, it was invented by our people, and then publicly circulated, it seemed pretty clear that that would hardly have been done if those responsible thought that months might still elapse before overt action should be taken by us.

Since I had come out of prison I had visited various men in different parts of Wicklow who had shown some enthusiasm for the Volunteers, but I had not had the opportunity of really getting new companies formed. On the days following that Wednesday I cycled around the county and saw those that I thought might really come out for the Rising, and told them to come in to me on the Saturday night, as I thought that by that time I should have pretty certain information if anything were about to happen. I also went into Dublin on those days, as I wanted to hear what news might be available. But I found little that was new, though the signs still indicated that anything might happen at any moment. Also ever since I had heard of the ship that was to bring arms I had anxiously watched the paper to see if there would be anything there that would have reference to it.

On the Saturday I was still cycling around to see my likely men, and late in the afternoon I went to call upon a man who lived not so far from Bray. He had been attending the Company Drills all the time I was in prison, and would now have a much better knowledge of the men than I had. I thought it very probable that I should have to put him in charge of the Bray men if it should happen that the Rising might take place while I was in Dublin. For that reason I took maps out with me and showed him the possible ways of getting his men into Dublin and told him to call upon me late that night as I thought I might find some message when I got home.

On my way home I called at the house where I had lodged when I first came to Bray. There I found two messengers waiting for me. One was a staff officer from Dublin, a particular friend of mine, and also of Blythe's and of the General Secretary of the Volunteers. With him was the General Secretary's fiancée. They were both very excited. They pulled me into a room and told me that the Rising was to take place the next day. That it was a perfectly mad enterprise. That the leaders who had made the plans seemed to have lost all common sense and to be acting in desperation. The General Secretary, who was also an officer of the I.R.B., had discovered the arrangements accidentally at a meeting of the I.R.B. and had conveyed the information to those members of the Executive who were still in the dark. He had now been arrested by our own people, and was held a prisoner somewhere, though they did not know where. The fiancée was in a state of great excitement, asserting constantly that they would shoot him.

The Staff Officer asked if my wife were back from England. I answered 'No'. He told me to telegraph to her to come back immediately. I pointed out that if she were coming that night she must be already on the train, and that I thought that was probably the case. If she were not, there was no boat until the following night. He then told me as a friend that I should be made to take my place in the Rising. I asked did he intend to stay out of it himself, and he could not answer that. But he said that in my case, I was married with two young children, and would therefore have a special justification in refusing to take part in an act that could do no good and must inevitably lead to my own death. That I should also see that none of the men under me took part. I pointed out that though I might do that with regard to the men in Bray and in County Wicklow, there were others in West Kerry who had been brought into the movement by me, and that I had no means of getting in touch with them. If I took his advice I might find that they had gone out as a result of my own teaching, while I stayed at home. He still urged me to stay at home. No one could blame me, he said, for refusing to take part in an act that was complete madness.

I asked was it absolutely certain that the Rising would take place on the next day (Easter Sunday). He said it was. Could nothing be done to stop it? Nothing he thought. When O'Rahilly had heard about it he had gone out to Eoin Mac-Neill's to see if anything could be done, but that was a forlorn hope. In the end I said that I should go in to Dublin in the morning and see him, and then decide what action (or inaction) we should take. In the meantime he and the fiancée were hurrying back to Dublin to see if anything could be done to get the General Secretary released.

When I got home I thought over the matter, and could not see how I could accept the advice to stand out from the Rising if it were really coming off on the morrow. I decided to go to the first Mass in the morning and then to meet the boat at

Kingstown to see if my wife were on it, to tell her the news and then to hurry into Dublin.

In the morning I went to the first Mass, and then on to Kingstown only to find that the boat was already in, and the passengers disembarked, and I could see no sign of my wife there. I expected to find her there as the first train for Bray had not yet gone and would not go for a good while yet. My position seemed to be desperate. I had left my house with the two young children in it being looked after by the daughter of my ex-landlady who had kindly arranged to stay there to allow me to go into Dublin. Now I felt that I should have to go back to make some arrangements about the children, and in the meantime the Rising might have already begun in Dublin.

While I was waiting on the platform I saw a man in Volunteer uniform and I thought that he might solve my difficulty. I went to him; told him that I was a staff officer of the Volunteers and that I wanted him to take a message to Bray for me. He explained that he was going off on some sort of Volunteer picnic. I tried to convey to him that things were happening that cancelled all previous arrangement, but he seemed to fail to see what I could possibly mean. I had presumed when I saw him in his uniform, that he had received a mobilization order and was actually going to participate in the Rising. When he finally realized that I was speaking to him as to an Irish Volunteer he pointed to the badge upon his cap, N.F. which meant that he was one of Redmond's Volunteers. I had forgotten that there was any such body.

Then the train came in. There was nothing for it but to take it back to Bray and see if I could make some arrangement there that would allow me to go off to Dublin and leave the children looked after. When I got out of the train at Bray I saw my wife. She had come on the boat, but as there was a train going to Dublin immediately she had taken it into town as she could have beakfast there with friends and still catch the first train to Bray.

I told her immediately that the Rising was fixed for that day. We rushed to the house to see the children, but they were not there. They had been taken to Mass by the friend I had asked to look after them. There was no time to wait so we caught the next train to Dublin. As we were hurrying to the lodgings of the Staff Officer who had brought me the news the previous evening I saw the placard of the Sunday paper. It referred to the ship of arms, which apparently was taken by the British. I explained its significance to my wife as we hurried on, and said that this was the last blow.

When we arrived at my friend's lodgings, his landlady said he was out. She did not know where he had gone, but the moment he had seen the order in the morning's paper he had hurried out. I thought that she must be referring to the news about the arms ship, but as she kept on referring to the 'order' I asked to see it. Then she showed me an official order from Professor MacNeill as President of the Executive cancelling the mobilization for that day.

We left there to hurry to O'Rahilly's to hear what was really the position. But just as we drew near his house I saw a taxi coming towards us, and in it were the Staff Officer and the General Secretary's fiancée. I hailed them. They stopped the taxi and the man got out. He told me that the order in the paper was official. He was hurrying to notify that to various officers and asked me to go to the houses of two men, one of whom was Cathal Brugha and tell them that the order was official and to convey that to their men. I asked no further question but hurried on. At the first house the man I wanted to see opened the door in uniform. I gave him my message, but he did not understand what I was referring to. I produced the paper and showed him the order. He still failed to see that it was of any great importance and I realized that he had no idea that the Rising had been timed for that day. I told him that he must get in touch with his men immediately and tell them of that order so that they would not mobilize. That he agreed to do. Then I went on to Cathal Brugha's. He was out. His wife told me that he was at 'the meeting' in Liberty Hall. I knew nothing about that meeting, and gave her my message which she did not receive too graciously. Then I hurried back to O'Rahilly's house. He was not there. He had gone down to Limerick with the countermanding order and had not yet returned. The Staff Officer and the Secretary's fiancée were there, pre-occupied with the plans for the release of the General Secretary. I decided to go to Liberty Hall.

When we arrived there there was a crowd outside and then a company of the Volunteers of the Labour Party came marching up and went into the Hall. One of them was one of the men who had been sentenced for taking material for munitions from the Railway works and whom I had met in Mountjoy. He came over to me, and I asked what was happening. He said that they had been out for a little march and were now 'ordered into barracks with rations for forty-eight hours'. I immediately interpreted that as meaning that the Rising was not abandoned.

Then I heard a woman in the crowd telling all those about her that she had come over with the boys from London, and that they were all ready and would be in it. Someone asked her what she was talking about and she replied with great surprise, 'What, don't you know that the Rebellion is coming off.' I dragged her on one side and without any polite formulae told her to keep her mouth shut.

I saw a motor car covered with dust passing along, and inside it was the O'Rahilly, his face white with dust, and looking dead tired. I hailed him and we got into the car. He was just back from his trip to Limerick and other places with the countermanding order. Though he was worn out he was very cheerful for he felt that at the very last moment the message had been got to the men in the country to prevent an abortive Rising. I told him what I had heard at Liberty Hall, from which I gathered that the Rising was not abandoned, but he did not take it seriously. He felt that a disaster had been effectively prevented. He was so convinced of that that we drove home to his house in a mood of light-heartedness. During the rest of the day people were continually coming with new reports, but the general feeling was that a disastrous attempt at a Rising had been escaped from at the last moment. There were some who seemed to think that the all important matter was now to arrange the release of the General Secretary. But when night came he was still unreleased and his whereabouts unknown. It was late when we went off. My wife was to stay with the Secretary's fiancée and I was staying with the Staff Officer who had brought me the news the previous day.

I shared the Staff Officer's room; our beds were at opposite ends of the room. As I lay thinking over the events of the day I became more and more convinced that the Rising would still take place. It had been this conviction at the back of my mind that had decided us to stay in town until we knew definitely what was to happen.

My room-mate was pre-occupied solely with the question of his intimate friend the General Secretary. As he lay in bed he seemed to become still more excited about this matter. It had been arranged that the next morning he and my wife and the Secretary's fiancée would take a taxi out to MacNeill's and bring him into town to summon the Executive and demand the immediate release of the Secretary. But the Staff Officer as he lay in bed began imagining that his friend might be shot, because, he said, the others would be in a state of fury that the Rising had been prevented.

I tried to reassure him on this point. It was absurd to think that he would be shot in any case. And, apart from that, I was becoming more and more convinced that it was impossible to arrange a national uprising to take place on a certain day, and to cancel it at the last minute and then go about one's day's work as though no such thing had been contemplated. I became so exasperated by what I considered to be the sickly imaginings of my room-mate, and his unfair statements about the men who had tried to bring off the Rising that we practically quarrelled. All that day I had been working with those whose one object

125

was to prevent the Rising taking place as arranged. But now as I thought it over it seemed to me that those men had known their own mind. And the others had let them go ahead and had asserted themselves only when it was in fact too late.

We did at last get to sleep, or at least I did, for I was completely worn out. I had got up at six o'clock on that Sunday morning. I had hardly a minute's rest all day, and only a piece of cake, an apple and a banana to eat.

I could have slept on in the morning but my friend called me and urged me to hurry up as MacNeill must be brought in as soon as possible. But it was more the prospect of breakfast that inspired my haste. The three weeks that I had been out of prison had not yet dulled my appreciation of non-prison diet. The landlady was just bringing in bacon and eggs when a Volunteer officer who had been with us the previous day appeared. He brought with him an envelope which to the best of my memory had these letters written on it, 'G.E.T.M.U.N.A.Y.' Whatever it was it meant, 'Mobilize your men at 10 o'clock for active service'. My friend immediately became excited. He jumped up from the table. 'The fools,' he said, 'they are still trying to go ahead with the Rising.'

My reply 'I told you so, it was inevitable at that stage,' did not appease him.

'We must get MacNeill immediately' he said, 'And O'Rahilly. We must get all the men who aren't mad and stop it. I'll get a taxi and go for MacNeill and you get O'Rahilly.'

I was loth to leave the breakfast that was now before me. But there was nothing to be done but to rise from the table immediately, albeit reluctantly.

Just as we reached the door of the house my wife and the fiancée arrived. They were also excited. They had been trying to get a taxi to take them to MacNeill's but had failed.

My friend said he knew a number of garages and would get one. Meanwhile I should go on and tell the O'Rahilly of the new developments.

I ran to O'Rahilly's. Although I knew nothing of the

geography of Dublin, I knew the way because I had gone just the same route the previous morning.

I arrived out of breath and perspiring. Madame O'Rahilly opened the door. On the previous night after that day of alarms and excursions she had said that if there was any bad news she did not want to hear it. But she now asked me what was on. I merely demanded where was O'Rahilly. He was still in bed, she said, as he had not slept while he was travelling with the countermanding order. I rushed up to his room. He was still asleep, but I caught him by the shoulder. He opened his eyes, and seeing me was immediately wide awake. 'Well, what's the trouble now?' he asked. 'The Rising is on this morning', I replied still out of breath. 'We have received the order "Mobilize your men at ten o'clock for active service."' At that he laughed. 'If men are determined to have a Rising nothing will stop them,' he said.

I then told him that the others had gone out to MacNeill's to bring him in to his (O'Rahilly's) house, to try to stop the Rising.

While we were still talking of this beside the bed we heard the others arrive. We presumed that they had MacNeill with them. But when they came into the room it was only to say that there was not a taxi to be got anywhere. The Staff Officer was quite satisfied that this meant either that they had all been commandeered by our people, or that the British had heard of the plans and had commandeered them. It was only afterwards that we learnt that this was in fact due to Fairyhouse Races.

The question was how was word to be got to MacNeill. I said that if I had a bicycle I would go out immediately. O'Rahilly said his bicycle was in the garage. But I wanted another one, because I knew that O'Rahilly's bicycle had a slow puncture and a number of other things wrong with it, so that it would just carry him, and he was much smaller than I was. He said that it only needed the back tyre to be pumped and it would then be all right. I then had to ask what roads to take, due to my unfamiliarity with Dublin.

I started off, peddling as fast I could. But when I reached the

127

village of Milltown I heard a burst, and looking round saw bits of rubber of the back tyre on the road. That finished the bicycle for me. I put it in a shop and then saw a milk cart going in my direction. The driver gave me a lift for a short distance, but he was only going a very short part of the way. Then I left the road and took a short cut by the Dodder to Rathfarnham. I thought that I should be able to get some conveyance there. I saw a shop with a notice outside that there was a jaunting car for hire, and went in to ask for it. But the man said that it was hired for the day, he was going to the Races. I thought that he might be a Volunteer and so I said very significantly that I wanted only to go out to MacNeill's, and that it was very urgent. He did not respond to the significance of my look, but said that if it was only to go to MacNeill's he could take me and still be back in time for his appointment. He produced the car and at last I got to my destination.

I told MacNeill my story but he was not impressed. Members of the Inner Circle of the Executive had been out with him during the week-end and had said that they would have a parade of the Volunteers just to show that the countermanding order did not mean that we were cowed. I tried to convince him that the order now was for 'active service', but he was still unconvinced. I then said that in any case I would not go without his agreeing to come in immediately. Even if I were wrong about the Rising taking place that day, he was still wanted in town to demand the immediate release of the General Secretary. At last he agreed to come in on his bicycle. He would go to the house of a friend in Rathgar, and we could get him there during the day.

I saw him mount his bicycle and I got on the jaunting car that had brought me. The driver was now in a hurry with his other appointment, and would not take me an inch past his own house in Rathfarnham. But from there I got a tram, and ultimately got back to O'Rahilly's, my journey having taken considerably longer than we had thought when it seemed that I should cycle the whole way.

I arrived at the house again out of breath and perspiring. Madame O'Rahilly met me. 'Michael has gone into town and taken equipment with him', she said. And with no more guidance than that I caught a tram into town. I suppose I thought that if the Rising was on I should be able to hear where it was. When I got to the corner of Nassau Street, I saw my wife near Trinity College. I jumped off, and her first words to me were 'It has begun. They are firing in the centre of town.' We both started off towards O'Connell Street. As we got nearer there were many people on the street and an atmosphere of excitement. People turned us back. 'You can't go along,' they said. 'It is held by military.' We took their word, and tried other approaches. But each time people told us that the road was held by military. I was in a state of despair. For some reason I presumed that our men were somewhere about the Nelson Pillar surrounded by military and just being wiped out. I had no weapon with me.

We turned back, and along the road I met a Volunteer in uniform and with no hat. He also presumed that we were cut off from our men by military. I told him to go to the house in Rathgar Road where he would find MacNeill and to tell him what he knew. I met another man, S.M. who also felt that he was cut off, and then another man I knew who had been in the Tralee Volunteers. S.M. said that he would go along by one way to see if he could find out what was happening, while we went another.

It seemed to be quite hopeless. I thought the Rising was probably already over, or about to be over, and there was I walking the streets quite helpless. We saw a restaurant open— it was of the sort that used to be called 'a good pull up for carmen'. My wife suggested that I should try to get something to eat there, while she looked around to see if there was any means of getting in touch with our men. The man I had known in Tralee came in with me. The proprietor seemed to be delighted at the prospect of our custom as there was no one else in the shop. We gave our order and waited for it to be brought, but just as the proprietor, all smiles, was coming with it, my wife rushed in to say that it was all right. Our men were in the Post Office, and there was nothing to hinder approach to them. She herself had spoken to them.

We rushed out of the shop leaving the bewildered landlord standing with the plates in his hand. As we passed Bachelor's Walk we saw Volunteers taking possession of a shop at the corner. We spoke a few words to them and hurried on. There was quite a crowd of people on the street. As we approached the Post Office we saw the Flag being hoisted over the roof, and Mr. Pearse standing on the street outside. It seemed almost impossible that this should really have happened. I said to my wife 'This is worth being wiped out for'. I made to go forward and found that the man with me was not coming. I told him to come along, but he said that he must send a telegram, and that he was due to take his position in the Rising in Kerry. I pointed out that Mr. Pearse was only a few yards away, and that he could get instructions from him. But he hurried off to see about the telegram. As my wife and I hurried forward Pearse saw us and came towards us with a welcome. He looked rather graver than usual. I felt that while he had something of elation there was also a heavy sense of responsibility. He told me that O'Rahilly was in the Post Office, that he was in charge of one side of the top part, and he appointed me O'Rahilly's adjutant.

CHAPTER EIGHT

The G.P.O.

We went in and were greeted by many friends. One man who was posted at a window with a rifle came forward to shake hands. I had met him on the ring in Mountjoy, where he had done a short term for assaulting a policeman. He had explained that as he always regarded policemen as renegade Irishmen, he always had a tendency to assault them.

While I was on the ground floor, two smiling Swedes came up. They explained that they had heard that we were fighting the English, and as they did not like the English they had come to join. But they belonged to a ship that was sailing on Thursday, and they would have leave to in time to catch it. They were also posted at one of the windows.

When I reached the top-floor O'Rahilly came forward. Still smiling, 'They were determined to have a Rising', he said, 'so here we are.'

'How long do you think we can hold out?' I asked.

'By a miracle we might last for twenty-four hours', he replied, 'but I don't think we'll go for that long.' I thought his estimated extremely optimistic. He took me around and showed me the part that was under our control. There were men on the roof and at the windows with rifles to shoot when we were attacked. There was the restaurant of the Post Office for the feeding of the men and a fairly large store of food. There were

131

a number of girls to look after the arranging of the meals and serving of the men. There were a few prisoners who had been taken when the Post Office was assaulted. Of these four were private soldiers, who had been in the Post Office as a guard, but, as I was told they had no weapons near them when our men entered. There was a lieutenant who presumably happened to be there just by accident. The four privates were very happy, apparently, and working hard. They had the advantage of knowing the whole geography of the building and could tell us where everything was. The lieutenant held a bottle of brandy which he was drinking in a state of utter gloom.

When O'Rahilly had shown me everything we settled down to try to establish some sort of order. We saw that the men were at their posts, arranged when and how they were to be relieved. We explored the place to see all ways of ingress and egress and so on. When we had it all settled I suggested that we had better make a report to the leaders below. But he asked me to do that. Then we talked. He thought that a great mistake had been committed in precipitating the Rising at that moment. We both agreed that it was only a matter of hours until we should be all wiped out. I saw that he felt that he had been treated badly by the 'others' and I agreed with him. I think I was more indignant at the way they had behaved to him than he was himself. He was just hurt. It was quite clear that they had not thought that he would be in the Rising when it took place.

At length I went down to make the report. I found that I had to report not only to Mr. Pearse, but also to Tom Clarke and to James Connolly. Mr. Pearse, as he looked at the men about him with their weapons—pitiful weapons to set out to beat the British Empire with, some were rifles, but more of them were shot-guns, and there were some that we called the Howth rifles, very antiquated—as he surveyed them I could see that he was deeply moved. These young men had come out at his bidding to give their lives for Ireland. He did not question any of the arrangements that we had made. I felt that he would hesitate to criticize any arrangement once we had come out in answer to the call. He spoke affectionately of the O'Rahilly. I could see that he felt that a grave injustice had been committed in the treatment which O'Rahilly had received from those he had worked with.

Then I went on to Tom Clarke. He was clearly elated that Ireland had indeed risen in arms, though so few were our numbers. He did not hide the fact that he had been and still was bitterly angry that the countermanding order had been sent out. But time and again he hastened to add that of all men he admired O'Rahilly. And I felt that he had good reason to do so. They had doubted if O'Rahilly really meant to come out and risk his life, and they now saw that in the service to which he was so devoted he was not only ready to give his life but to give it under the command of those whose action had imposed upon him a mortal insult. I asked Tom Clarke as I had already asked Pearse, what prospects were before us. But in both cases I got no definite answer. Tom Clarke digressed immediately to say what a fight we should have put up if no countermanding order had been given. But he did not by any means say that even in that case it would have been a victorious fight, or even a fight whose outcome could conceivably have been in our favour.

I could speak less freely to James Connolly. I had not known him before. I felt that it would take very little to make him angry.

As I moved about in that lower part of the Post Office I saw another prisoner who had been taken. He was a policeman who had been stationed in the Post Office. Apparently somebody had decided that his safeguarding would be simplified if he were deprived of his boots. He now sat clutching a bottle of Guinness, the removal of his boots revealing that he wore grey socks which needed darning very badly as both his heels and both sets of toes were thrust out through holes. As I approached him he looked up at me, a picture of gloom. I felt sorry for him, as I presumed that we would all be killed and in the final assault his prospect would be little better than our own. But the few words that he uttered between his groans indicated that he was

133

not anticipating that to-day's events would cut his life short but rather that it would detrimentally affect his future career.

When I got back to my own part of the building I found Volunteers who had come up for food telling the girls that the Germans had landed troops somewhere. The number landed was given sometimes as ten thousand and sometimes as twenty thousand. This information was accepted as a certainty. They assumed that those troops were marching on Dublin, that more troops would be landed and that victory was certain. I was depressed and distressed to see them talking of victory, when I was quite satisfied that in a matter of hours they would be called upon to face inevitable death. I tried to discourage these rumours. But they could not be killed.

The next time I went to Mr. Pearse I told him that I objected to having those under my orders filled with false hopes by false rumours. He quite agreed with me. I said that I wanted to tell them the most hopeful thing that was known for certain. Was there anything that suggested that we were getting outside help? He told me that smoke had been seen in the bay and that they honestly believed that there were submarines there. I asked was that all, and he said that was all. It was little enough, but still it was more than I expected.

When I got back to my own part of the building I found that the lieutenant had finished his brandy, was now very drunk and demanding another bottle. In our survey of the stores we had seen that there were two bottles of brandy and when I had reported that to Mr. Pearse he had said that they were to be kept as the Red Cross people might require them for wounded men. I therefore told the lieutenant that there was no more brandy for him. In any case I should have refused to let him have more, for he was now stupid and unable to stand steadily on his legs. I thought that when the end came his one chance of being saved was that he should have all his wits about him and be able to make his identity known to the attackers before he was shot down. He constantly came to me asking for more brandy, even with tears in his eyes. And of course I refused.

It was only long afterwards that I realized that he wanted to drown his senses because he was in a state of utter terror.

Just after I had dealt with him another man came in with a truculent air and shouted to me, 'I want a bottle of stout.' In that same survey of stores I had seen that the only alcohol we had was the two bottles of brandy. I heard afterwards that before I came there had been stout, but apparently some puritan had done away with it. I told this man that there was no stout, but that did not convey much to his mind.

'I'm one of Jim Larkin's men,' he shouted, 'is there no stout for one of Jim Larkin's men.' I told him that as there was no stout at all there was obviously none for Jim Larkin's or any other men. But he only shouted the more. Finally he raised his voice and announced to the world at large 'I want a drink'. I then quite maliciously asked him why he had not said that before and called a girl to bring him a glass of water. At that he nearly burst. He wanted no water, he wanted stout. I told him that he could come in and see for himself that there was no stout there, and that then he would have to get out or we should have him removed by force. At that he departed gurgling with discontent.

Some time that first day Mr. Pearse came to me and giving me some money told me that food had been commandeered from various places without being paid for. He asked me now to go to those places with the young man who had done the commandeering and to settle the accounts. One of the places was the Metropole Hotel. When I approached the Manager there and he saw that young man with me, he immediately became angry and said that that young man had assaulted him on his earlier visit, by taking hold of his arm. He was now determined to charge him with assault. The young man denied that it was an assault, and the two of them began arguing. Meanwhile, another man kept clutching hold of me and telling me that he represented the *Dispatch*, that if I would care to make any statement to him he would promise that it would be published exactly as I made it. At the same time he besought me to give him a copy of our Proclamation. Meanwhile the Manager clutched me to say that he was not going to accept the treatment that he had received but would take action against the young man with me. When I tried to tell him that I had merely come to pay him for what had been taken, the newspaper man pulled me away to beseech me to make a statement. In the end I told the newspaper man that if he did not leave me alone I should put him under arrest, and when I had him quieted, I brought out the money and asked the Manager to take what was owing to him, and as to his taking action against the young man, he was quite free to do what he liked about that, but the young man was pretty well certain to be shot before the day was out and so was I, and the Manager himself would be better advised to take steps to see that no bullet reached himself, instead of worrying us with threats of a fine or a few days in gaol.

Somehow, now that the Rising was a reality it was the amusing side of every incident that impressed my mind. It was only when I had time to think, or was speaking with O'Rahilly or Pearse or Joe Plunkett that the overshadowing tragedy became real.

At the same time there was much that depressed me. I have forgotten whether it was that first day or soon afterwards, but I remember standing outside the Post Office with Mr. Pearse. I knew that the apparently inevitable fate of all of us weighed heavily on his mind, but I knew also that he derived consolation from the thought that Ireland had again risen in arms, and that his own life would be given in the service of her people. But we could look along the street and see the 'people' surging into shops and looting. I was overwhelmed by the thought that the sacrifice he was making meant no more to them than that the sanctions of ordered society were toppling over and gave them a chance to enrich themselves with stolen goods. Pearse stood beside me looking down the street at them, and there was tragedy written on his face. All his own nobility and his sacrifice of himself and those poor souls that followed his lead weighed as nothing in the scales against the opportunity it offered to go home with a sackful of boots. I asked were those caught looting to be shot, and he answered 'yes'. But I knew that he said it without any conviction. And some time later a prisoner was actually handed over to me charged with looting. When I reported this to Pearse and asked what was to be done, he replied: 'Ah, poor man, just keep him with the others.'

Again O'Rahilly would come along to talk to me. He agreed that once the preparations for the Rising had been pushed ahead a certain distance it was unthinkable that he should not take his place in it. But at the same time he was quite convinced that it was badly timed, and he could not be satisfied that a real justification existed for leading those young men out to die. And at the back of his mind was the knowledge that he had left a devoted wife and family to give his life in an action that not only had not the assent of his own judgment, but that had been decided upon by men who treated him as he had been treated. They had treated him as of no account and yet at their words of command he had no option but to give his life supporting them.

When the men or girls about me talked about victory, and about a future after the Rising in which they should be alive I again felt depressed. In one way and another I shared responsibility, and their talk made that responsibility weigh heavier upon me. If they of their own choice had come out to certain defeat and death it would have been a very different thing from coming out because they thought that their leaders had chosen to act with a view to victory or probable victory. Of course to my mind defeat meant that those who were not killed in the fight would be duly executed afterwards. I was so convinced of this that one time when O'Rahilly wanted to give me the address of a man who was in no way connected with the national movement, but who by reason of some relationship would take me in if I succeeded in escaping when the final assault came I laughed at the idea and did not even take down the address.

O'Rahilly used to take some sleep at nights, but I did not. I remember that on the Tuesday morning he came into where I was, and I greeted him with the words:

'Why I thought we were to be wiped out yesterday.'

He laughed. 'So we should have been. It is against all the best military rules that we are still alive.' And then he added more seriously, 'But don't worry, it is not going to be put off for long.' Every morning while the Rising lasted, I greeted him the same way, but as the days went by it was less light-hearted.

Bad news began on the very first day. When we had entered the Post Office, Mr. Pearse told us of the buildings that had been seized. Among them he mentioned Dublin Castle. That seemed wonderful to me. In all the uprisings in Ireland Dublin Castle had remained in the English hands. He then asked my wife to take a flag to be hoisted over the Castle. But some time later she came up to our part of the building with a different story. She had hurried to the Castle taking it for granted that our men were in possession. She was hurrying in at some entrance when she found bayonets pointed at her. She thought that it was one of our men on guard and looked up to assure him that it was all right when she found herself facing soldiers dressed in khaki. She hurriedly turned about. The attempt to take the Castle had failed. In our Rising as in those of previous centuries Dublin Castle remained in the enemy's power.

We had men in various buildings around about the Post Office to cover the approaches, but they gradually had to fall back to our headquarters.

Practically every time I went down to the big hall on the ground floor I stopped and spoke to Joe Plunkett. He looked appallingly ill but at the same time very cheerful. Then, probably on the Monday evening he came up to my part of the building, looking like a dying man. 'I must have a rest,' he said. 'Can't you sit down and let us talk.'

I told someone to bring him food and sat down with him. Though he looked like a dying man he seemed to be supremely happy. We talked about our friends, many of whom were due to take part in the Rising, but we did not know where those who were not in the Post Office might be. Then he went on to give me a long account of a visit to Germany. I found it intensely interesting. I was enormously impressed to know at first hand that we had actually negotiated with a foreign power. I remember thinking to myself that if it were not for the fact that I should never leave that building alive I should make notes of what he told me. But as it was it seemed quite pointless that I should make mental notes of his story. There were many details that I meant to ask him about, just because of my own personal interest, when Mr. Pearse came and joined us.

I felt that he also was exhausted and that he wanted rest. We even tried to talk about unrelated things, but it was impossible to abstract our minds from the circumstances of the moment. I was firmly convinced that it was only a matter of hours until we should all three be dead, and I was also sure that they both shared that conviction with me. I certainly could not ask Mr. Pearse how long he thought we should hold out as I had asked O'Rahilly. He talked of the Rising as a glorious thing in itself, without reference to what it might or might not achieve in the light of the position at that moment. Both he and Plunkett spoke of how much bigger an event it would have been had the original plans gone forward unchecked. But they did not suggest that even in that case we might have expected a military victory. The very fact that the conversation returned so steadily to what might have been was an admission that there was no doubt now as to what was going to be.

I could not ask why a date had been fixed and persisted in when there was no help forthcoming from outside, beyond the ship of arms that had failed to land its cargo. Whenever that ship was referred to Mr. Pearse was careful to repeat that the arms it had contained were not a gift. That they had been bought and paid for either by or through our own people in America. The reiteration of that point in the circumstances of that moment seemed to me to be significant in establishing that the Rising was our own work without any outside participation. It did not

answer the questions that were in my mind. But as even while
we spoke of indifferent things Pearse's face revealed that his
mind was occupied with the burden of responsibility that lay
upon him. I could not voice my questions. I agreed heartily
that in all probability what was then happening would revivify
the spirit of Irish Nationalism which had seemed to perish at the
declaration of War. Provided that that faith lived on, when the
mutations of history brought, as they ultimately must bring,
the favourable moment, the Irish Nation would be ready to
seize the occasion and to spring into life.

Again the talk went back to what might have been and with
the assurance that the arms that had been sent were a purchase
that our own people had made, and that the Germans had done
no more than to try, unsuccessfully, to send them to the pur-
chaser without even attempting to send a voluntary support, it
seemed to me that if they were apparently so indifferent to our
success now, when by helping us they might well recognize that
they were helping themselves, and when our success might
well make the difference between success and failure for themselves, then there was still less assurance that in the hour of their
victory, if they were to be victorious, they would put themselves out to make the satisfaction of our demand for freedom
a condition of the peace that was to follow the war. I therefore
asked Mr. Pearse what interest the Germans would have in
coupling our demands with their own when and if the hour of
their victory came. In putting my question I did not relate it to
the fact that the Germans had made so little effort to assist us
at that moment.

Both Pearse and Plunkett hastened to put forward the theory
that even in the event of German victory, the Germans would
still have to look forward to possible dangers. Obviously they
would not attempt to annex England for to do so would merely
create for them a permanent source of weakness within their
own system. Neither would they attempt to annex Ireland for
that would merely make us a weakness to them as we were
now to England. But they would need to see that England

should not be able to challenge them again in the immediate future.

In those circumstances it would obviously be good policy for them to take steps to establish an independent Ireland with a German Prince as King. They even named the Prince, Joachim. In those circumstances they would have an Ireland on the far side of England, linked with them in friendship flowing from the fact that they had promoted that independence and from the link of royal relationship.

That would have certain advantages for us. It would mean that a movement for de-anglicization would flow from the head of the state downwards, for what was English would be foreign to the head of the state. He would naturally turn to those who were more Irish and Gaelic, as to his friends, for the non-nationalist element in our country had shown themselves to be so bitterly anti-German. Such a ruler would necessarily favour the Irish language, for it would be impossible to make the country German-speaking, while it would be against his own interests to foster English.

For the first generation or so it would be an advantage in view of our natural weakness to have a ruler who linked us with a dominant European power, and thereafter when we were better prepared to stand alone, or when it might be un-desirable that our ruler should turn by personal choice to one power rather than be guided by what was most natural and beneficial for our country, the ruler of that time would have become completely Irish.

Talking of these things that might conceivably have been may seem to have been more calculated to depress us, seeing that even while we were speaking we were conscious that when the assault came it must necessarily overcome us. But somehow they cheered me, and it was quite evident that Pearse and Plunkett found comfort in speaking of what might have been.

Those talks between the three of us were repeated at various times during the week. No matter what might be happening when Pearse and Plunkett came in I went to them immediately.

In spite of Plunkett's cheerfulness and in spite of the fact that I thought that every one of us in that building had at the most a few days to live, my feeling that Plunkett was a dying man inspired me with a great pity for him. I could not look at Pearse's face without being moved. Its natural gravity now conveyed a sense of great tragedy. There was no doubt in my mind that when he looked round at the men and the girls there, he was convinced that they must all perish in the Rising to which he had brought them. And having decided both for himself and for others that they should sacrifice their lives for the Irish people, he knew that those who had been out about the streets on various errands came back and reported that the people were ready to attack them. And he had seen how the people had seized the opportunity that he had given them to loot the shops, and were too preoccupied with their own cupidity to give a thought to the fate which he had chosen for himself and his followers.

Plunkett could forget in conversation, the facts that surrounded us. Sometimes when there were only the two of us together we would talk about literature and writers, and he would ask questions about writers who were friends of mine. But with Pearse it was different. Even when he spoke of what might have been, one felt that the major part of his mind was turning over what actually was. Time and again we came back to one favourite topic which could not be avoided. And that was the moral rectitude of what we had undertaken. These can hardly be called discussions for only the one side was taken. We each brought forward every theological argument and quotation that justified that Rising. And if one of us could adduce a point that the other two had not been aware of it was carefully noted. I remember asking to have such points repeated and for exact references. One of the reasons for this was that in talking with others this question so often arose, and any quotation that seemed to be authoritative and that favoured us, was comforting to the questioners. During those talks I probably persuaded myself that we were only interested in being

142

able to give some reassurance to others. But looking back since then I know quite well that as far as I was concerned I was also seeking for reassurance for myself. Certainly none of the three gave voice to any argument that might call the rightness of our action into question, unless it was that we had an immediate refutation ready for it.

I would rise up from such a conversation to be met by a man with a note from a subordinate officer that was dated the 1st (or 2nd etc.) day of the Republic. The mere sight of those dates at the head of such notes angered and depressed me. It depressed me because I not only felt quite certain that those days were numbered but also that that was the last day. I was depressed to think that the writer of the note was so blandly blind to the reality as to think that those days were to continue indefinitely, and to forget that our ordinary method of computation referred to an event in time that was about to be of far more moment to him than the decision to take up arms on the Monday morning. And that method of dating seemed to associate the Rising with the French Revolution, an association that was utterly repugnant to me.

It was fairly early in the week that Pearse asked me how long the food would last. I asked how many men we had there to provide for. He said 'we have a little over two hundred'. As a matter of fact I knew nothing whatever about such matters, but as the feeding of the garrison was in my charge, it was natural that I should be called upon to give such information. But it so happened that I had a girl working on my staff who had already shown that she was an expert in such matters. I presumed that her ordinary work must be associated with a restaurant or an hotel. She was an Irish girl who lived in Liverpool and who happening to be in Dublin for a holiday, had volunteered her services to us. [Her name was Peggy Downey.] I asked her if she could give any computation and she immediately impressed me with her expert knowledge. She counted up the stores and could say exactly how many men could be fed with a loaf, a ham or any other food, and for how long. She then worked out a sum and said that we could feed two hundred men for three weeks provided that we exercised the most rigid economy. I did not dream of questioning her calculations, and duly reported to Mr. Pearse.

'Then exercise the most rigid economy,' he replied, 'for we may need it for three weeks.'

I certainly did not think we should need it for anything like that length of time, and from the way he spoke I thought that he very much doubted it himself. But as it was a conceivable possibility, I gave the appropriate orders. The result was that I was quickly regarded as completely heartless. A great many of the men for a large part of the day and the night would have no particular duty assigned to them, and for want of anything better to do would stroll along to the restaurant to pass the time eating and talking together when they had finished eating. Apart from the fact that this was incompatible with the rigid economy that I had been ordered to establish, they prevented other men from getting a place to be fed and created a congestion that made any order impossible. I learned afterwards what I suspected at the time—that in my endeavours to remedy this, men who were exhausted after long hours of arduous work without food, were bundled out together with those who had been in and out of the eating room all day and night. Mick Collins, whom I knew by sight, without knowing his name, and who had quickly shown himself as the most active and efficient officer in the place, strode in one evening with some of his men who were covered with dust and had been demolishing walls or building barricades, and announced that those men were to be fed if they took the last food in the place. I did not attempt to argue with him, and the men sat down, openly rejoicing that I had been crushed. Apparently some of them had already been the victims of my rigid economy. But while they were eating those of our most regular and assiduous customers who appeared at the door of the room were told to disappear quickly or they would be dealt with.

.　　　　.　　　　.

I noticed a marked collapse in the general optimism one evening which I think must have been the Wednesday (though it may have been the Thursday). O'Rahilly and I went around as usual to see that windows of the various rooms were all properly manned. The men were at the windows looking out at burning buildings. They spoke with quiet voices as though they did not want to exclude the roar of the flames. They felt as we did that these fires were the beginning of the end. When we made our last round we saw that the fires were steadily growing, at least it seemed so to us. I said good night to O'Rahilly, and though as usual we made a few jokes together they certainly lacked spontaneity and sparkle.

Then as I was on my way downstairs a Miss C. came and asked could she talk to me for a while. At the very early stages of the Rising she had come to me and asked what hope I thought there was and I had told her none. I had learned from her that she had not been in the women's organization, but that her fiancé was a captain in the Volunteers, and when she knew that he was in the Post Office she had come also to be near him and to give what help she could to the cause that he served. We sat together on a box.

'The fires are terrifying,' she said. 'I am in a state of utter depression, that is why I want to talk. What do you think is going to happen?'

I told her that the only doubt that had ever been in my mind had been how long we should last.

'And do you think that all these young men will be shot?'

I knew that she was thinking of her fiancé, although she was in the same peril as he was. I wanted to say something that would give her some ray of hope. But I was so absolutely convinced that there would be but one end to all of us that I could not conceal my certainty.

'I think they will,' I said.

'I wouldn't mind it for myself,' she said, 'but it seems terrible that all these young men should be sacrificed, and they don't realize it.'

When I left her I went to the room where my prisoners were. I had given orders that a big fire should be made in the grate in that room to comfort and to cheer them. When I went in one of the privates who had been in the Post Office when our men took it came up to me and asked could he have a word in private with me. I moved off with him to hear what he had to say.

'Could you put us in a different room?' he asked.

'This is the best room I've got for you,' I said. 'What's wrong with it? Look at the fine fire you have. There's nothing I'd like better than to stay in there myself.'

'It's not the room I mind,' said he, nodding over towards the lieutenant to whom I had refused the brandy. 'It's the sight of that fellow. When I do look at him I do be ashamed of being a man at all.'

I looked over to the man he indicated and he certainly did appear to be in a bad way. I went over to him.

'You shouldn't keep us here,' he said. 'Look at those windows. There is no protection. If you were shelled from this side we shouldn't have a chance.'

Some time earlier I had discovered a sort of basement or cellar with a vaulted roof, in which sacks of straw or waste paper or shavings were stored. I offered to take him there and he seemed grateful, but just then the other lieutenant prisoner came along.

'You know you have no right to keep me at all,' he said. 'I've told you that before. I am an R.A.M.C. man, and my work is looking after my patients. It is against all the rules that you should hold me.'

'I know you've said that before,' I replied, 'and you know what I said to you. What is the good of going over it again.'

'But you know, I believe in having a grievance,' he said, and I saw that he was pulling my leg as usual.

'Very well,' I replied, 'I'll make you an offer. Nobody can expect me to worry more about your troubles than I do about my own. You shall be with me all the time, and so you will be just as safe as I.'

146

(Photo: Irish Independent.)

Arthur Griffith.

(Photo: Irish Independent.)

Michael Collins, leaving the Treaty Debate in January 1922.

'Oh no, you don't get away with that. You've asked to be shot. You must like it, but I don't, you've got to look after me properly.'

I told him and the other man to come along and I'd show them the safest place I knew. He and I went off together with the other poor soul following on behind. I was whispering to my companion most unflattering remarks about the man behind us.

'You are not treating him fairly,' he said to me. 'You know he is in bad health. He was here undergoing treatment and you made a prisoner of him.'

I showed them the cellar that I had found and pointed to the solidity of the roof, and explained all its points. The invalid officer seemed really to accept it, but my R.A.M.C. friend condemned it roundly. It was not fit for human habitation.

'Well there it is,' I said. 'It's the safest place I've found. If you find it uncomfortable, you don't have to stay. I'm not shutting any door on you.'

But when I moved off, the R.A.M.C. man came along with me. I think the other man stayed there for a while, and then went back to the room we had come from.

I told the R.A.M.C. man that as he wasn't staying there the best thing he could do was to come with me to look at some wounded men I had. There were two bad cases. One man I had brought down from the roof, thinking that he was about to die. He was shot through the eye, and bleeding from a wound in the throat, so that I thought that he must be shot through the throat. But I afterwards found that that wound was only from a cut made by a bullet as it fled past him. The other man was wounded in the abdomen with a large wound in the back.

We had no qualified doctor on our staff although there were a couple of medical students acting as doctors. When my prisoner had examined the patients he turned to me and said.

'These two men should not be kept here. They should be taken to hospital immediately. It is impossible to keep those wounds from being infected here.'

But as he spoke he was looking after the men.

'What's the good of talking about taking them to hospital,' I said. 'We can only do the best we can for them, and the best I can do is to get you to look after them.'

But I went off to tell Mr. Pearse what he had said.

As time went on the fires around about us increased, and the roar of the flames grew. In talking to my chiefs I felt that there was no longer any point in avoiding reference to the end that approached. I even found it easier to talk to Mr. Connolly. At the earlier stages I had always felt when I went to talk to him that he was likely to round on me and rend me. I had gone to see him one time when he seemed to be in a furious temper. I gathered that he had given an order that someone was to lead out a body of men to bring something in, and it had not been done. He appeared to think that the man had been afraid to venture out, and shouted to the men to follow him. Shortly after that he was carried back wounded in the hip, and thereafter he lay upon a stretcher. Now when I went to him I felt that I was received in a much more friendly way. I don't know why, but before that I had assumed that he viewed anyone who was not associated with the Citizen Army as only dubiously well-disposed. But now when I went to speak to him as he lay upon the stretcher, probably in considerable pain, he would keep me there talking over things. We even talked of the difficulty there would be in moving him, when the end came.

On the Thursday morning, Tom Clarke called me and took me out to a yard to show me a concrete opening like a room, and told me that I was promoted (though I wasn't sure what rank the promotion gave me) and that when the end came I was to gather all the girls I could in that shelter, and defend them to the last.

'It means,' he said, 'that if you are not killed beforehand, that you will be taken by the enemy and probably executed.'

After that exciting Wednesday of the previous week,* when

* *Ed. note*: When Bulmer Hobson had spoken against a Rising at a meeting.

I had gone to bed I had had a nightmare in which I thought that I was hanged, and after being hanged I could see myself, without any head and my body suspended from a hood that went through my throat. That dream was very vivid with me afterwards. I was obsessed with a horror of being hanged. This had been very much in my mind ever since the Rising began. I was really anxious to be shot in the fight, lest, failing that, I should have to face the gallows afterwards.

As soon as Tom Clarke said that this new proposition made it likely that I should be taken by the enmy, the one thing that was in my mind was whether that meant that I should be shot or hanged.

'What do you mean by executed?' I asked. 'Does that mean hanging or shooting?'

'I should think they will probably shoot the men they take,' he said, 'but they may keep to the hanging. The English love hanging.'

'But can't you say for certain?' I asked.

'No, but I should think it would be shooting after a Rising like this, and in the middle of the war.'

I accepted the job he gave me, though I was far from feeling happy about it. I even took occasion to speak to Joe Plunkett and Mr. Pearse to ask what they thought would be done to men taken prisoner. They were inclined to think that the worst would be shooting, but at the same time they thought it possible that it might be hanging. Nobody seemed to think that it mattered at all what way a sentence of death was carried out. They certainly did not realize that to me that was the all important question!

Now that one could talk quite freely about the approaching end, I went to Mr. Pearse and said that I thought that it was ridiculous to keep with us the girls who were looking after the feeding of the men. They were serving food upon plates, washing up dishes and cutlery and doing many jobs that were not strictly necessary. It is not comfortable to eat without a plate, but the amenity of plates was hardly worth sacrificing lives for. I said that as the girls would all be killed if they stayed, they should be ordered to leave the building. They might be killed in doing so, but at least it gave them a chance to escape that they would not have if they stayed on.

Mr. Pearse did not question my gloomy anticipation of the end, and agreed that they should be ordered to leave. He told me to get them all mobilized, dressed for going out first thing the next morning (Friday) and that he would give them the order.

Before making this proposal I had discussed it with two who had shown themselves outstanding in efficiency and devotion to work. One was the girl from Liverpool who was expert in all matters relating to the feeding of men [Miss Peggy Downey] and the other Miss G.D. [Miss Louise Gavan Duffy]. Miss G.D. had worked unceasingly day and night. She had not only not slept, but had hardly sat down. She had been well-known in the women's organization before the Rising began, but when she had reported to me, she made no secret of the fact that she felt that our position was at least doubtful from a moral point of view. Nevertheless, as the Rising had taken place, and as the men were there in arms, she felt that it was her duty to come and do all that lay in her power to ameliorate their condition. She certainly would not have taken up arms under any circumstances. Her sense of humour was keenly alive. She was apparently completely devoid of fear. She remained perfectly calm, no matter what danger threatened.

These two agreed with what I proposed, but suggested that they themselves might remain behind when the others went. They had in fact made themselves indispensable. And Mr. Pearse had observed that and agreed that they should stay on. But, he said, they should appear to leave with the others, or none would go. They were to dress with the others and to march out with them at the end of the column, but when they had gone a little distance they were to slip back again.

That night I announced this decision to the girls. They protested against any special care being given to their safety, but

I said that such were the orders of Mr. Pearse, and that for whatever little time longer we might hold out, it would be a simple matter to forego the more civilized forms of serving food. Some of them suggested that they might be added to those who were attached to the ambulance section. I think one or two were actually transferred, but it was clear that if more went to that section they would be more in the way than useful.

In the early morning I took them to Mr. Pearse. They all had their hats on ready to go. When they were before him he made a speech. I myself was moved as I listened to him. He said that the Rising was the greatest armed attempt by Ireland since '98. They had obeyed the call to come, and now the order to go was equally binding upon them. He said that there was the possibility that they, or some of them, might be shot after they left the Post Office. But they had shown their readiness for that when they took up their positions.

It was natural that his speech should have moved many of them to tears even if there had been no other cause of grief. But implicit in Pearse's words had been the implication that the end was now approaching. They were going off, leaving those with whom they had shared danger, and who would probably not survive the end that was admittedly now so near.

Just as they turned to go Sean MacDermott came to say that they should not be ordered to go but merely told that they were free to go if they liked. The girls were not out of hearing distance. It seemed to me that Mr. Pearse hesitated as to whether to change the order. Sean MacDermott's argument was that in ordering the girls out we might be ordering them to immediate death.

I feared that his interposition would only make a new disorder. And I hastily interposed that the girls had received their order and it should remain. If they went now there was a chance that some might be killed, but on the other hand they might get safely home. But to stay meant that they would all inevitably be shot. And if the order they had received were withdrawn, all would stay. Even if my proposal had been bad, it would be worse to create confusion now by changing it. Mr. Pearse agreed and they went off. I waited with him until the two at the end of the column returned as arranged. In a couple of minutes they were back, and within another couple of minutes they were working as hard as ever. I did not attempt to hide from them or myself that it would have been impossible to manage without them.

Later in the day I was informed that the Post Office itself was now on fire. O'Rahilly who was something of an engineer and expert in doing things with his hands went down to see what could be done. Some time after that I was with him. He had a hose in his hand and was shooting the stream of water up what seemed to be a very wide lift shaft. He explained that the water was not going high enough to put out the fire. I was down with him frequently, and each time he reported that the fire was winning.

At a later stage Mr. Pearse came and told me that the Post Office was to be evacuated. Food was to be prepared for the men to put into their knapsacks. It was to be placed in a heap in the big hall below, so that they could take it and fill their knapsacks as they marched past. Meanwhile he told me that I was promoted. He was quite unaware that Tom Clarke had told me the same thing before. At first I thought that the new situation meant that I should not be committed to falling into the hands of the enemy. But Mr. Pearse went on to explain my duties. The main body would leave by the door leading from the main hall into Henry Street. Meanwhile men were to go ahead with breaking holes through walls until they reached as far as a Music Hall which I think was called the Coliseum. I should be responsible for getting the wounded men, and any others that remained through to the Music Hall. There I was to put out a Red Cross Flag and then see if the wounded men could be got to Jervis Street Hospital. 'You must try to get them there,' he said, 'but I think it is in the hands of the enemy.' That was quite a blow to me.

He went on to say that I should try to collect any that did not go with the main body, and this would include some who would be on the roof to cover the evacuation.

Then I spent my time between seeing that the food arrangements went forward, and seeing how the passage through the houses was progressing. Finally, I was told that the food was already in the main hall. I saw that more than sufficient had been prepared for the men, and still there remained an enormous amount in our part of the building. I had to laugh as I thought of the rigour with which I had refused more than a bare minimum to the men through the week, and made them detest me, only to leave the most of it here to be burnt.

The wounded men were on stretchers, and as a new hole was broken through a wall they were passed through. The R.A.M.C. prisoner was with them, and a medical student who had volunteered on the Monday morning, as well as those who were part of our ambulance brigade. Most of the wounded men were strapped to the stretchers, but the most serious case, the boy who was shot through the eye, was merely lying on the stretcher with a rug over him. The R.A.M.C. man had apparently given him some drug that made him half-unconscious. He lay there with a crucifix in his hands. And as he was passed through the holes in the walls, he slid from the stretcher, groaning in his half-unconsciousness. I doubted if he would live through the day.

It occurred to me that as the enemy could see that our headquarters was on fire and would know that we must evacuate it, they would have their machine-guns levelled on the door out of which the main body of our men would go, so that they would just march out into a hail of bullets. And as we had now by breaking holes in the walls penetrated to a fair distance from the Post Office I thought that it would be a good idea if all the men were brought through those holes, away from the fire, and then when they finally went out into the street, the British would have no idea from what part they would come.

I went to propose this to Mr. Pearse. When I entered the main hall the men were gathered there. One could hear the noise of the fire. A crowd were by the piled up food filling their knapsacks or trying to get near enough to do so. There was an air of excitement and some confusion. Many of the men were armed with shot-guns with hair triggers, and as I tried to pass over to Mr. Pearse, first one and then a second wounded themselves in the foot. I stopped to cut off their boots and to have them sent after the other wounded men. These two shots going off in the middle of the hall seemed to add to the confusion. I looked over to Mr. Pearse who stood near the Henry Street door. He stood there with tense face. I was filled with pity for him. When the two men had shot themselves in the foot he shouted an order that all shot-guns were to be unloaded, but he had to repeat it to be heard. I remembered that only that morning I had been indignant with Sean MacDermott for suggesting that an order should be changed after it had been given, as I knew that it would create confusion. I realized that if now, just as the evacuation was beginning, a sudden change was made there would be utter confusion. Even if what I had in mind to propose was a better plan, it was better to adhere to the arrangements made rather than throw everything into worse disorder. I turned back.

O'Rahilly came to me to say good-bye. He was in charge of one of the bodies of men to be evacuated. He clasped my hand —'Good-bye Desmond,' he said. 'This is the end now for certain. I never dreamed it would last as long. The only thing that grieves me is that so many of these lads are good Gaelgeoiri (Irish speakers). But never mind, when it comes to the end I'll say—"English speakers to the fore, Irish speakers to the rear, charge." ' Then as he turned to go he said with a smile— 'But fancy missing this and then catching cold running for a tram.'

There were tears in my eyes as I left him. We had been bound together by the most intimate friendship. That friendship began in carefree days when we shared our love of the beautiful countryside of Kerry, and shared our dreams of a new and heroic spirit of Irish nationalism that was about to come into being. Now it ended with the city on fire about us and in a building already on fire, with, as we assumed death waiting for us when we left that building. He had shown his readiness to give his life for Ireland as anyone who knew him as I did knew he would do. But the joy of that sacrifice had been marred by the knowledge that those with whom he worked and with whom he shared his hopes thought that a consideration of his personal safety would influence his decision. I felt that he was the most tragic figure in that tragic gathering of men. He was devoted to his wife and family with a rare devotion, but he had decided to leave them to serve Ireland even when the call to service came from men who were revealed as not having realized how ready he was to give all for his country.

As I had now decided not to suggest my change in the plans as already made I had to give my attention to carrying out the instructions that I had received. The work of making a passage through the houses was being pushed ahead. I remember in one house where the men were breaking the hole through the wall there was a bag of dried figs on a table. The medical student recommended them to me, and half absent-mindedly I began eating them. I had hardly eaten all the week and it was only when I began eating them that I realized that I was hungry. The R.A.M.C. man was there. About a year afterwards a man who was in prison with me received a letter from one of those who were present on that occasion. The writer said—'Remember me to FitzGerald; the last time I saw him he was throwing figs at an R.A.M.C. man.' Apparently I must have been concealing my inward misery by an outward frivolity, or I may have been trying to make a show of cheerfulness to react against gloom in others.

During this time I was passing between where these men were working and the Post Office. Miss G.D. [Miss Louise Gavan Duffy] remained there until the very last. I suppose that she was still preparing food until all the men of the main body had left. Each time I returned to our headquarters I seemed to find more unattached men, whom I directed to the passage out through the houses. I was also making trips to the roof of the Post Office where men were covering the retreat, and they were to join up with us when that was done, or when their own escape was threatened by the fire, which was advancing all the time.

At last the passage was broken through to a house that had a window opening out over some roofs that led to a window in the Music Hall. Telegraph wires passed over those roofs, and for a time I stood there warning the men who carried the stretchers to duck their heads under the wires. Then I went back to the Post Office. Miss G.D. was now down below. As, on those last return journeys, it appeared that part of the route that we had originally used was already more or less invaded by the fire, I had made an alternative way by coming over some roofs when I got near to the Post Office, and then descending into a yard by means of a primitive ladder that was lying about. I had discarded my coat, waistcoat, collar and tie as I had been engaged in fairly heavy physical work. Now, as we climbed the ladder and got on the roofs I remembered that I had left some pound notes in the coat pocket. My first reaction was to go back for the coat that contained them. The fire would probably have made that impossible in any case, but just as the impulse to retrieve my wealth flashed through my mind, the futility of worrying about a few pounds or many pounds when I was about to make my exit from the world where they have value also took possession of my mind.

I made another journey to the roof. Dusk was now beginning and it was turning chilly. What seemed like small shells were dropping. I presumed that they were incendiary as they seemed to burst into little flames as they struck the roof. One of the men there handed over to me a raincoat that he was wearing. Then we made our way down, across the roofs, through houses then across the other roofs and in at the window that led into the Music Hall. That window led into what must have been a restaurant or bar. The medical student who never lost his sense of humour got behind a counter and offered to act as barman.

My instructions were that this place was now to be a Red Cross hospital and that the Red Cross flag should be hoisted out of a window. Before doing so I again asked if any of the men had arms, as I understood that it would be regarded as treacherous for us to have arms under the Red Cross flag. A few revolvers were handed up, but then I saw that our people had stored explosives in that place. There were bombs and fuses and grenades.

I found, or somebody gave me, two bolster cases, open at both ends like tubes of linen. My idea was that we should use those as bags for carrying back the explosives and weapons. But I knew nothing about bombs and did not know that they might not explode by mere contact together.

One of the men who had been shot in the foot and who was now with us was known as an expert in explosives. I therefore turned to him and asked him whether I could drop the bombs in the cases without their exploding. But it seemed impossible to get an answer from him. He handled them, as I thought, lovingly. In desperation, I took a coil (it was probably fuse) held it out of the window, and said that if there was any danger about it he had better speak quickly, as I was going to throw it out. As he did not speak I threw it out, and of course nothing happened. Then I took bombs and told him he had better say if it were dangerous to pile them into the bolster cases, and as he made no demur I piled them in. Then I asked for two men to take the two bags of bombs, etc., back as far as possible away from us. Nobody seemed to listen, but a priest who had been in the Post Office at the end to hear confessions volunteered and he and I climbed out of the window with the bolster cases slung over our shoulders.

We went back some distance through the houses until we seemed very near to the fire, and there I put the cases in some sort of sideboard in a room. As I was doing so, the priest called to me to look out, as there was a bomb that might be struck by one of the bullets that were flying about. I looked round to see where it was and then found that it was a tin of peaches that stood on the table, that he took for a bomb as our men had used such tins for making improvised bombs. During this time a bullet did strike the framework of the window (the glass was already gone) and enter the room, and a little splinter of wood just struck the side of my neck. I did not know this at the time, until I found that it was bleeding over my shirt.

It had now become much darker. When we got out from the window to cross the last roofs we both sprinted to avoid bullets. I remembered the telegraph wires and ducked, but the priest collided with them in the dark and had a fall.

When we got back to the other men, being now satisfied that we should not be contravening any international law by doing so, we put out the Red Cross Flag. We then settled down for a while, but I had in mind that our orders were that we were to try to get the men to hospital. This was reinforced by the fact that the R.A.M.C. man insisted that it was absolutely necessary that we should do so in order that the wounded might have proper treatment. It was also clear that we could not keep them there for long, as the building we were in was bound to be caught up by the fire.

We found that it was possible to get out into Princes Street which is on the other side from Henry Street. From there there was a passage leading into Abbey Street, and someone who knew the geography as I did not, said that Abbey Street was the way to the Hospital that the men should be taken to.

There was a barricade in that little laneway and it was on fire. But it was still possible to take the stretchers across, as the flames could be pressed down with a long box that was at hand, as the men were crossing. We did this and so found our way to Abbey Street. There were some bullets coming along the street but we kept close to the side and made our way along.

The R.A.M.C. man and the priest went ahead and signalled and shouted to a guard that was at a barricade near the hospital and negotiated for permission to bring the wounded men along.

We went forward and were taken into the hospital under the rifles of the British soldiers. Now I thought the end had come. Nuns (as far as I remember) decided that Miss G.D. [Miss Louise Gavan Duffy] and Miss P.D. [Miss Peggy Downey] (the expert on food matters who came from Liverpool) should stay the night there. I suppose that the soldiers were under a non-commissioned officer who did not know what should be done about the rest of us, for they sent for an officer who was probably a patient in the hospital. He came, with a flesh wound on the side of his face. I expected that that was to be the end of us, and so did Miss G.D., as I could tell by the look on her face as she left us. But when the officer came he said that the priest and the R.A.M.C. man should stay there and as for the rest of us we had better get back where we came from. They would give us two minutes to get out of the line of firing before they recommenced shooting along the street.

CHAPTER NINE

Escape and return home

Now for the first time since the Rising had begun, I felt that there was some remote possibility that we might escape. We hurried back to where the little lane led off the street that would give us shelter from the bullets. But it now seemed that just as I began to have hope the others were inclined to despair. I asked those who knew anything about that part of Dublin (and it was the very centre of the City), if they could tell of any way of joining the others. They could tell me nothing. Of course I knew that O'Connell Street was just at the end of Princes Street where the Post Office was and that normally one could walk round the Post Office to Henry Street. But there the fire was raging and there we were pretty sure to be mown down by bullets. No one could tell me of any other way. They were exhausted and hardly able to keep awake. They could only suggest that we should go back to the Music Hall. We therefore crossed over the burning barricade again and re-entered that building. It was quite clear that we should not be able to stay there long as it was too near the fire. However, we went back and settled most of the men to rest. The two men who seemed least overcome by weariness and disheartenment were the medical student and the friend who had given me the raincoat. One of them agreed to stay awake in a corridor and watch for fire, while I took my place in the dress circle and kept watch there.

160

I felt sure that there must be some way out to Henry Street, but if I left my post to go exploring I was not at all sure that I should be able to find my way back in the dark. I do not know how long we were there. But it did not seem very long until someone in the corridor outside called out that the place was on fire.

We hastily gathered the men together, and went out again to Princes Street. We moved on to the end farthest from the Post Office. Here it was a cul-de-sac. We succeeded in breaking into the building at the end (Arnotts, I think), but again this would only give us a temporary respite. We were in complete darkness. One man had a torch, but it flashed on for a minute only and then went out as the battery was exhausted. I raised my old plea that there must be some way out to Henry Street, but no one knew the way. If we broke up our party it was likely that we should never find each other again. In the end I felt about in the dark, getting one man to hold another's hand in a row. Then I numbered them off, told them that they could sleep and that I would watch to see when the little laneway was threatened to be cut off from us by the fire.

I waited until it seemed that the fire had practically reached that way of escape, and then called the men. I tried to make sure that they were all there, by calling the numbers and asking each man to step forward when his number was called. But I did not get far before I reached a number to which there was no answer. I was now in a state of very bad temper. I went on with the other numbers and when I reached the last and asked if there was anyone there who had not answered, I found there was another. I asked what his number had been and he said that he could not remember.

We climbed out into Princes Street again, on to the little laneway and then to its other end at Abbey Street. Bullets were coming along that street, and so we waited. I noticed that there was a certain rhythm about the shooting—after every little while there was a momentary lull before it began again. Then I saw a door on the far side of the street open and some people peer out from a house. I said to the men that I would give an order to charge and that at that order they should sprint across to that house. When the lull in the shooting was due, I gave the order and no one moved. They said that it was madness as they would only be shot.

I felt hopeless. The fire was advancing behind us. I rounded on the men and told them that it mattered nothing if we were shot crossing the road as we were certain to be shot in any case, if we were not burned to death. I told them that I would go across myself and they could do what they liked. I calculated the time for the next lull and shot across to the house where the door was open. The people in the house seemed quite delighted to see me and gave me a welcome. I stood talking to them in the doorway, but as soon as the next lull came all the other men came across like arrows out of a bow.

As they all pressed into the doorway the people became terrified. 'You'll get us all shot' they said. But now that we were all safely across I gave but little heed to our involuntary hosts. I put some of the men in the next house and kept the majority of them in the house we had entered. On the top floor there was a landing with a big skylight over it. Having disposed of the majority of the men I took the medical student and the man who gave me the raincoat, and said that we would settle ourselves on that top landing, where I could watch the skylight and judge when the fire approached.

An old man came out of a room on that top floor and was very solicitous about us. He brought a rug and insisted that we should lie down under it and take some rest. We did so, but I had no inclination to sleep. From time to time, I climbed up to the skylight to note the advance of the fire. As the dawn came large pieces of red charcoal were pouring down on to the glass. Then when I looked out I saw that the opposite side of the street was a roaring furnace. A wine and spirit store was burning there.

My two companions and I went downstairs and out through the garden to see what way of escape lay that way. At the end of the garden was a lane (South Lotts) and on the other side of that were the doors of stables. We went along trying to force

162

Liberty Hall, headquarters of the Citizen Army, after being shelled during the 1916 rising.

(*Photo: Irish Independent.*)

(*Photo: Irish Independent.*)

Arthur Griffith and Michael Collins.

our way into one of these, but it was clear that we should need tools to break down the doors. Then the people from the other houses began to flock out there. I talked to some of them and gathered that a woman who came from a house a couple of doors from the one we had taken shelter in was named Madden. We went back and got the men together. I told them that there was a big crowd out in the lane at the back from all the houses, and that our one chance was to join with them as though we were just the same as they were. I warned the men that they should see to it that they had nothing with them that would reveal that we came from the Post Office.

We all went out and joined with the people, though at the same time we were holding little consultations among ourselves. I remember that I noticed that one man still had the breeches of a Volunteer uniform, and I told him to slip back in to one of the houses and get another suit from the wardrobe of one of the householders. I myself picked up from the road a cap that had probably been dropped by a looter and put it on my head.

A little to the left of the house that we had left there was a turning leading from the lane to the Quay. Some of the people went along to that lane and signalled to the soldiers who were on the other side of the river. They were told to march up to O'Connell Street and then cross the Bridge and then along the other side of the river to where the soldiers were. I could see nothing else for us to do but to go with them, for the fire was behind us and driving us forward.

We went across to the military. We were lined up while the soldiers searched us in a desultory fashion. We were accepted as the inhabitants of the houses driven out by the fire. The search was concluded and the officer in charge was just telling us to go our ways, when a sergeant pointed out an antiquated revolver that someone had slipped out of his pocket and put against the wall. I took it for granted that it must have been one of our men who had been too sleepy to listen to what I had said more than once since we left the Post Office.

When the officer realized that one of the crowd had been armed, he changed his mind and lined us up and marched us all to Trinity College. We were put against the railings of the Bank of Ireland, to await our turn to be examined by an officer who was under the porch of Trinity. We squatted on the ground, and as I talked there to the medical student I put my hand in my pocket and drew out some slips of paper. They were notes that I had received during the week, most of them headed 'such a day of the Republic'. I tore them up, and slipped them inside the railings, realizing that I was guilty of the very stupidity that I had condemned in the others.

Then we were led across the road and taken inside the gate of Trinity. As the officer under the porch finished examining one, a soldier called in another. Some were held and some were told that they could go. As I waited I tried to invent some story about myself that would sound convincing. But I realized that I was too exhausted to think out a coherent lie that I would not contradict under cross examination. Therefore when I was called in and the officer asked me my name I told him 'Fitz-Gerald'. He asked me my address and I gave him the address in Bray. He looked it up in Thom's Directory that he had beside him, and found it there. He asked me where I had slept the previous night, I said in Abbey Street. He asked what house, and the name of the people I stayed with. I told him that I could not answer that. It was a house a couple of doors from Mrs. Madden's. I had taken refuge there as the streets were swept with bullets. Finding that the house and the neighbouring houses were threatened by fire early that morning I had called the people and come out on to the lane at the back of the house, and that was how I came to be brought there. He asked me what friends I had come to Dublin to see, and where I proposed to go now.

That was an awkward question. I knew no one in Dublin except through my association with the movement, if I mentioned MacNeill or the O'Rahilly, I presumed that their names would be known to him and would be sufficient to condemn me.

But I thought that as O'Rahilly's sister had her husband's name, that would sound quite innocuous to him. I therefore gave her name and address, as the house I was about to go to and the one I had visited when I came to Dublin from Bray. He looked up the address in the directory and again he was satisfied.

During that time a non-commissioned officer had been searching me. Now just as the officer showed that he was completely satisfied about me, the soldier called attention to the fact that the cap I was wearing was quite new and that it still had slips of paper gummed to the lining telling the price and the size. He also called attention to the fact that under the raincoat I had not a coat or waistcoat. This made the officer suspicious. He asked me to explain. I pointed out that as I had already told him, I had hastened out of a building that was threatened with fire. In my haste I had not even donned coat or waistcoat. Even the raincoat did not belong to me. I had got that from a man in the street, and the cap I had picked up in the roadway. I cannot hold out my statement as a pattern of truth. Far from it. But my caution in not trusting to my inventive powers had really put me in a position to make my story hold together under questioning. The officer said to me 'You can go', and then told the soldier to call in the next for examination.

I walked straight to the gate. The guards there hesitated to open it for me, but the soldier shouted that I was all right and I was allowed to go my way.

I knew my way to the O'Rahilly's sister's house. But when I went to turn round into Nassau Street, only a few yards from where I had been examined, I found myself facing bayonets held by two soldiers. 'You can't pass along here' they said.

There was nothing for it but to try to keep the direction in my mind and to see if I could get there by making a detour through streets that one was allowed to pass along. I therefore went on along Grafton Street, and avoiding every place where I saw uniforms I ultimately decided that I was really moving in the direction of the house where I had slept with my friend the Staff Officer on the previous Sunday night. But as I came to

165

what I afterwards knew to be 'Kelly's Corner', I again found two bayonets threatening me. They were held by two soldiers and with them was a sergeant.

I assured them that I had just come from Trinity College, that my name was FitzGerald, and that if they rang up Trinity they would be told that I had just come from there. But the sergeant was not at all convinced. He took hold of my hand. It was black from the time when I had stood on the burning barricade pressing down the flames while the wounded men were carried across. Indeed I must have looked a brigand. I had not shaved since the previous Monday morning, and it was now Saturday. My hair was long. I had not had it cut since I left prison. Under the raincoat I had no coat or collar or tie, and on one side my shirt was stained with blood.

The sergeant lifted my hand to his nose and smelt it. I have no doubt that it smelt of fire and smoke. He looked knowingly at me.

'Keep him there, if he moves shoot him. I'll get an escort from Portobello,' he said to the two soldiers whose bayonets were touching my raincoat. Then he went off.

The soldiers remained with their bayonets pointed at my body, and I stood in front of them. But after a minute or two, when the sergeant had disappeared I said, 'You can shoot if you like, but I am very tired and must sit down,' and I sat on the pavement with my back against the wall of the shop that they occupied, and they did not shoot.

Other soldiers were going in and out of the shop, and standing about. Two civilians came along and were halted but then a civilian came out of the shop and went over and said to the soldiers, 'I identify these men as two Jews. Let them pass', and they were allowed to pass. This man then stood at the doorway and I entered into conversation with him and the men who were guarding me.

Then a baker's cart appeared and halted some distance up the road. A non-commissioned officer called some soldiers to go with him to commandeer two dozen loaves. As the bread was taken into the shop, I saw my guards looking at it with hungry eyes.

'Can't we all go in and have something to eat,' I said. And the man who identified the men as Jews, said to the soldiers, 'Yes, bring him in and give him something to eat'.

They immediately agreed. We went down a flight of steps to a basement. My two guards set about getting food for themselves and took no more notice of me. There was a sink in the room, and as no one bothered about me I went over and washed my face and hands. Then a friendly corporal came up to me and began speaking. He originally came from Rathmines, he explained. He went on to talk about what was happening in the City, and I complained that it was impossible to get about without being held up with bayonets. I also complained about being detained. It seemed to me that he had a good idea that I had been in the Rising and wanted to help me.

'It's your hair that makes them suspicious, you know,' he said. 'They say, long hair, a crank; a crank, a Sinn Feiner. You'd be all right if you had it cut.' Then he took me into another room, and got something that was like a scissors, but not exactly a scissors, and began clipping off a certain amount of my hair. Then he got a narrow blanket from the bed of some soldier (assuring him that I would return it) and folded it to make a neckerchief for me to conceal the fact that I had no coat, collar or tie under the raincoat. Then we went back to the other room. Just then a man in a uniform that seemed to belong to the sea, came limping in with a wound in his foot. His remarks seemed to be merely variations of one obscene word, but he must have mingled others with it, because I gathered that he was anxious to meet one of the rebels and that when he did he would deal very severely with him, for the rebels were guilty of wounding him.

I put him on some sort of couch, or it may have been on two chairs, demanded a knife, cut his boot off and ripped up the leg of his trousers. I then demanded boiled water and a clean piece of linen. Men rushed to get the water boiling on a stove, and someone produced clean handkerchiefs which I dipped in the boiled water and bound around the wound.

Just as I was doing this, with the soldiers about me obeying my orders, an officer came in. He asked what was wrong, and I explained that the man had a wound in his foot, that I had only bound it up aseptically, and that it would want proper treatment. The officer spoke to the wounded man and then turned to me and said what a worrying time it was. He had a sister living in Rutland Square and he could get no news of her. The city was on fire and for all he knew she might be burned to death.

I then told him that I had come from Trinity College and that there were people there who said that they had come through Henry Street (I had heard that at Trinity) whereas I had been in Abbey Street which was on fire. I therefore inferred that the fire was more in that part of the city and would not yet have got near to Rutland (Parnell) Square.

He said that was reassuring, but he was still worried. As he began moving towards the stairs I went with him, still assuring him that I was quite convinced that the fire was not near his sister.

When we came out through the door he was just shaking hands with me, as I indicated that I was going, when the sergeant arrived with the platoon from Portobello. He was obviously annoyed when he saw me going.

'Are you letting this man go?' he asked.

'Yes, why not?' said the officer.

'Do you think he is all right?'

'Yes. Don't you?'

'No I don't,' said the sergeant, but he obviously felt that he could not stand out against his superior.

I turned to the officer. 'That is the way it is everywhere', I said. 'One is stopped at every corner. Couldn't I get a pass or something?'

'I have no authority to give any,' he replied. 'Of course I know you are all right, but you'll have to take your chance.'

168

He shook hands with me again, and I set off diagonally towards a corner across the street. The corporal inside had tried to explain to me the places to avoid if I got out, but I knew too little of Dublin for that to be much use to me, but I had gathered from him that the other direction (towards Rathmines Road) was one to be avoided.

But when I went to turn the corner I was again met and challenged by men with bayonets. I looked back and saw that the officer was still within sight so I called to him and he told them to let me pass. At that time I did not know that the road I was entering was Charlemont Road, but I knew from its direction that it was running parallel to Rathmines Road and therefore taking me towards the lodgings of my Staff Officer friend.

I did in fact reach his house without further interference. I knocked at the door and it was opened by a man who was presumably the landlady's husband, but I had never met him and he had never seen me. He had an anxious look, which became still more anxious when I asked for my friend.

'He's away,' he said. 'He went away days ago and we don't know when he will be back.' I could see that he felt that his lodger was in danger.

I was wondering how I could convince him that I was in fact a friend, and not coming to arrest his lodger, but he was far too suspicious. Just then I observed that at the back of the hall his wife was peering out to see what was happening at the door. I hailed her by name and she hurried forward and pulled me in and shut the door. They both explained that they were momentarily expecting the military to come to search the house for my friend, who was indeed away somehwere, though they did not know where he had gone. In fact they had thought that he was probably with me in the Post Office.

I told them that I wanted a complete outfit of clothes and the means to shave. I had already noticed that the ends of the legs of the trousers that I wore had got burned as I stood on the burning barricade. I also said that I wanted to look through my friend's papers for some addresses. This last request was because when we had arranged for the bringing back of Blythe I had told my friend that he must get together some addresses of unsuspected people who would receive him when he came back, and I presumed that there would be such a list somewhere in his room.

The landlord brought me hot water, razor etc., and I shaved in great comfort. Then I looked through my friend's wardrobe for clothes, and what I did not find there I got from his landlord. The latter and his wife kept coming into me full of anxiety as they were quite sure that the military would arrive at any moment.

I found the list of addresses, which was rather disappointing as it only contained two, and of those one was that of the house where I had lodged when I first came to Bray, and where the people were known to the police as friends of mine. The other address was of a girl named Greta living not very far away from where I then was.

I said good-bye to the people of the house and started off for the address I had found. I discovered the house without difficulty and knocked. A lady came to the door again with an anxious face. I asked for Greta. She immediately told me to come in and shut the door after me. In the hall she said:

'You've been in the Rising. You come from Mr.—.' I was surprised that she could know this when I had merely asked for her sister. But she explained that no one called her sister Greta except my friend. Therefore when I said that name they knew that I must have it from him.

Greta and another sister were in the room they took me to. They all wanted news of the Rising. They felt that it was all over and that we were defeated and I could only confirm that. They also thought that their house would be searched, but they did not anticipate that there was immediate danger of that. Greta said that she would take me to two girl friends, who would be able to suggest a place for me. At this stage of course,

I had completely accepted the idea that escape was possible for me.

But as we sat there a company of soldiers came along the road led by an officer who seemed very excited, and although the road was quiet, he suddenly shouted that there were snipers and he indicated the direction of the house we were in. It looked as though he and his men were about to come to search for snipers and so Greta and I slipped out without delay.

We went to the house where her girl friends lodged, but they were out at Mass, and to await their return we went into Palmerston Gardens and sat on a seat there. I remember noticing that the others in the park were two couples who were apparently much in love. A passing surprise occupied my mind that when death was in the air young people were still making love. I pointed out to Greta that we two sitting there would obviously be thought to be like the others rather than that I should be taken as a fugitive. And in a few minutes we took on very much the appearance of the others, for now I felt the exhaustion of almost a whole week without any rest, but constant hard work and strain. I began to doze and my head fell upon her shoulder. She remained unmoving and silent to let me sleep until she thought that her friends would probably be back at their lodgings.

We went to their house. They had not returned. There was no certainty as to when they would come back as apparently they had gone off somewhere else when they left the church.

Greta now made another suggestion. She knew a priest in a certain monastery [Mount Argus] who was a strong supporter of ours. She would take me to the monastery and ask him to take me in. Now I was so tired that I was ready to accept any proposal. We started off and went into the church belonging to the monastery. It was now Saturday afternoon, and people were kneeling there going to confession. I knelt with the others while she went to a door at the back of the church and asked for the priest she knew. I saw her talking to him at the door, and then she came back to me.

171

'It's all right,' she whispered. 'He'll take you in that door. You'll be quite safe here.'

She took me across and introduced me to the priest and then she said good-bye.

Just as the priest was about to shut the door after us a woman stepped forward and asked to speak to him. He told her to wait a minute and he would be back. Then he put me in a room and went to her.

When he returned to me he said, 'Did you know who that lady was.' I replied that I did not.

'That is Mrs. Pearse,' he said, 'Padraig's mother. She wants to know if I have heard anything about him, and if there is any chance for him.'

I could only say that I thought there was no chance. What chance was there? If he was not already shot after leaving the Post Office, it was certain that the British would not rest until they had captured him. And if that happened I did not think that there was any likelihood that he would be spared. I wanted to go out to see Mrs. Pearse, although I knew that I could say nothing that would give her hope in her great grief. But the priest advised against it.

When he came back to me he brought another priest with him. They told me that the superior of the monastery had not shown himself as a supporter of ours, and therefore they would not let him know that I was there. They would be able to keep me there until the morning, and then I could slip out of the church with the other people after the first Mass. At that moment I was too sleepy to give any thought as to where I should go when I slipped out after that first Mass. I told them that all I wanted was somewhere to sleep. They considered together and then took me through various passages and ultimately put me behind the organ in the Church. I promply lay on the floor and slept. But in a few moments one of them came back with rugs to wrap round me. I thanked him and promptly slept again.

Later on I was wakened again by one of them. He told me

that it was now night. The church was closed. The first one to enter it in the morning was a caretaker or verger, and they were afraid that I might be breathing heavily or snoring, and if he heard that he would raise an alarm. It was therefore proposed that I should go to an empty room belonging to one of the priests who was away for the remainder of the night.

I followed my guide down to that room. He told me that he would call me in the morning so that I could slip out with the people who were at the early Mass. I now explained to him that I knew very little about Dublin, and knew nobody except those who were most implicated in the Rising. Where should I go when I left there? He gave me an address.

As arranged I was called in the morning, entered the church through the door from the monastery just before Mass was over and went out with the people. I found my way to the house I had been recommended to, but when I explained my case to the owner he was dismayed. He was occupied with a lot of various maps of parts of Ireland. He wanted me to go off immediately without waiting to say any more. I countered this by asking where I was to go to. He said that he had already injured himself by his enthusiasm for the revival of the Irish language, now he was expecting ruin, and my presence there made that ruin certain. He pointed to the maps. He had them out with a view to destroying them as they revealed his interest in Irish topography which apparently would be prima facie evidence that he was associated with rebellious movements. I indicated that I had no intention of leaving there until I had some idea as to where I was to go to. He seemed to have in mind that I had been followed to the house and that armed men would burst in at any moment.

Then his wife came in. Her attitude was very different. She also showed anxiety, but it was only anxiety for me. She set about reassuring him, and she seemed better qualified to do that than I was. She was going to Mass. She would see two people whom she named to her husband, and arrange that I should go to them. Meanwhile I was to wait there until she came back. The unfortunate husband had perforce to agree to that. While she was gone he and I sat and talked, with a kind of friendly demeanour that was utterly devoid of any pretence at geniality. I was quite conscious that I had to leave that house.

At last his wife returned but she had been unsuccessful. Whether it was that the people she had expected to see had not been at that Mass, or whether there was some reason that made it impossible for them to come to the rescue I have no idea. We discussed what was to be done, always assuming that I could not stay there. At last, in sheer weariness I said that while I was about it I had better call on MacNeill and let him have my report of the week, as I had reported to him on the previous Monday that the Rising was to take place. But I did not know how to get to him. Neither did I know what places should be avoided as likely to be held by military. The lady of the house offered to come with me. Her husband insisted that she should not go beyond a certain place that he mentioned, as after that the way would be straightforward to me.

She and I set out, but she did not turn back at whatever spot it was that her husband had mentioned. We went on to Rathfarnham, but the arrangement was that we were to go in through the grounds to the Castle and there ask for a certain Mr. O'L. and then ask him to let us out through the wicket gate as by that way we should avoid having to walk through the major part of the village. We did that, came out of the wicket and so along the road to MacNeill's.

We approached that house carefully as we thought it quite probable that the military would be there before us. But as we saw no sign of uniforms we went up to the house. Of course I knew that this was not a house that I should choose to stay in as it was certain to be visited by the British Authorities fairly quickly. When we went in I found not only Professor MacNeill, but the General Secretary of the Volunteers, who had been arrested by our own people before the Rising began, and his fiancée, and my friend the Staff Officer whose clothes I was wearing, and another member of the Executive who had opposed the Rising.

They were all horrified at my going there. They thought I must be mad, as they were waiting to hear the cars bringing the military along. I insisted on giving an account of the week, and took quite a long time telling my story. Then I said that I would go over the mountains to the house that we had occupied the previous summer and in which there were people I knew now living.

I really had in mind to make my way right over the top of the mountain, but when I had gone some distance I found I was too tired, and came back on the road that leads through the mountains to Glencree. I knew that this was dangerous, but my mind was numbed with weariness and it seemed not worth while to worry about safety. It was only a matter of being captured sooner or later.

As I went along that road I found people standing by the roadside. Seeing me coming from the direction of Dublin they asked me for news. Was the Rising over. I said I thought it probably was. They said they hoped it was ended one way or the other. They had been unable to get stores from town during all the week. I smiled and told them that I thought they would soon be able to get what they wanted now.

Then further along I saw a girl who had been a servant to the people that I was now going to call upon. She just stared at me in bewilderment. Her name was Emily. Whenever her mistress had called her it reminded me of a line of Chaucer, 'Alas mine hertes queen, alas mine Emily', and therefore I had always referred to her as 'Mine hertes queen'. So I just said as I passed her on the road 'Hullo Emily'. She said nothing but continued to stare as I went off along the road. I learned afterwards that word had come out that my body was lying in Dublin with exactly twenty-six bullet wounds and therefore it seemed to her that she was seeing a dead man walking along, and saying 'Hullo Emily'.

When I arrived at the house I was making for it was already

dark. I knocked at the door and the lady of the house came out and peering in the dark she asked 'Who is it?' I told my name. She also had heard that I was dead, but my presence did not make her speechless. On the contrary she seemed only delighted that I was really alive. Soon afterwards her husband came in. He also was astonished and caught me in his arms with delight. I felt to myself, this is the first house I have met where they seemed glad instead of terrified at my presence.

I think we must have sat up most of the night. Though I don't know why we did, unless it was that there was so much to say. I do know that if I got any sleep it did not seem to be sufficient for me, for the next day I sat in an armchair and slept steadily. But it was not an unbroken sleep. There were three elderly ladies who lived a few miles off, who came to the house. They had always been supporters of ours, and now they were running about feeling that everyone was going to be arrested and shot. They kept calling at the house to say that it was going to be raided. My hostess would come in to tell me what they said, but as she told the story afterwards, I merely opened one eye and said, 'Tell them to go to Hell', and went to sleep again.

Of course I realized that it was quite possible that they were right, that the house would be raided. In fact I took it for granted that every house that seemed at all likely to contain anyone associated with the Rising would be searched, that is to say any house whose occupants had any association with those who were likely to have been in the Rising. And my hosts were certainly known to have been friends of mine. If I could have thought of a house where I would be received and that was not likely to be suspected I should no doubt have planned to go there, but I could think of no house, save my own, where I was likely to be welcomed. Those who had been well disposed towards us before we actually rose in arms, now showed every desire to be dissociated. I could therefore expect nothing from those who had been uninterested or hostile. My reaction to a warning that the house I was in might be searched left me in the position that any house I could think of was still more likely to be searched. And that house had the advantage that its owners had really been glad to see me, and my hostess still seemed unconcerned about any danger that I might be bringing to her. But I noticed that that was not the case with my host. The constant alarms were telling on him. He would go out, and return in a little while more and more convinced that a raid was imminent, and to his earlier concern about what might happen to me I saw that there was now added a concern as to what the finding of me there might mean for himself. As that Monday advanced I saw that I should have to move on from there. I saw signs that my host would ultimately make it clear to me that no matter where else I might go I must leave his house. The best that I could hope for was that I could stay there until after dark, and in the meantime the best thing I could do was to take things easy.

As I lay in my armchair going from doze to doze I tried to think of some comparatively safe place to go to but I could think of none. I saw that I should have to make for home, and see if I could arrange from there for someone to receive me.

Some time in the afternoon I was conscious that there was a visitor. There was whispering in the hall, an excited feminine whisper, and shortly afterwards I saw a woman's form passing the window going away. My hostess came in to tell me that it was a certain Protestant lady of a family that was traditionally Unionist who had called. As she had begun to walk straight into the room where I was, the lady of the house had dragged her into the kitchen and there bluntly told her that I was asleep in that room. Naturally she had only done this because she was satisfied that she could be trusted. Indeed the Protestant lady instead of being hostile had immediately become excited and alarmed about my safety. She had hurried off to see if she could get any information that might be useful to me in my position.

Some time after that I heard hurried feet passing on the gravel outside the window and caught a glimpse of that same visitor practically running to the door with a red face, the result of her haste. This time she burst straight into the room where I was.

'Run, run' she said. 'They are coming up to search this house, I have news from the police.' My hostess appeared behind her in the doorway, now definitely alarmed. I tried to ask questions, but could get no answers, except the cry of 'Run, or you will be too late.' The visitor had five pounds in her hand that she was trying to press upon me. Even as I was going towards the back door she was trying to press this on me, but I turned and said, 'It is no good to me; I am only going up into the field behind. There is no place to spend money.'

The field behind was the beginning of a mountain, rather wild land, mostly covered with furze bushes. I was probably not at all convinced that the lady had any real grounds to think that the house was going to be raided, and in any case there was nowhere else for me to go. If the police did come and search the house there was the chance that they would not make a thorough search of the furze bushes on the hillside. In any case it was more dangerous for me to appear on the public road as I should have to do to reach any other place where I might conceivably find a shelter.

I made my way up the hillside, and then settled down in the midst of a cluster of furze bushes that completely concealed me and from which I could keep a watch on the house. Lying there I could see that no police or military turned up. And I stayed there until dark fell. I had now made up my mind that I could no longer return to that house as a lodger. In any case it seemed to me that a real escape was impossible. The most I could achieve would be to postpone capture. I therefore decided that I should try to make my way home. There at least I would be welcomed. If I were captured there, it made very little difference, in fact it was rather better than being caught somewhere else which would only bring trouble on others. At the same time at the back of my head was the idea that my one hope was that from my own house some arrangement might be made with friends that would make a permanent escape possible.

The darkness fell completely and still the house had not been raided. I had worked out the route that I would take to get home through the least frequented roads and passing the fewest houses. Then I heard the back door of the house I was watching open and my hostess came out bringing a lantern. I thought at first that she meant it was a signal to me, but she came up on the hillside after a cow that was grazing there. I rose up out of the furze bushes and went towards her. She had not lost her courage in the least. I told her that I had made up my mind to try to get home. She was concerned about the danger of such a decision, but she could suggest no other place, and she said quite frankly that her husband had been affected by all the warnings and that he would certainly not want me any more in his house. She joked about the wild women and their alarms, but could not conceal the fact about her husband, and indeed we both had to recognize that it was a fact that the house might indeed be raided, in which case I should be captured if I were there, and her husband would be involved as a result. In any case, she insisted, I must go in and have a cup of hot cocoa before I started on my walk as I was shivering from lying for so long on the hillside.

I thought I noticed that my host's face fell and that a look of anger came over him when we went in, but it was immediately explained to him that I was about to go away as soon as I had had the cocoa, and then he became himself again and concerned about me.

I said good-bye thinking that it was very unlikely that I should ever see them again, and moved by the thought of the welcome that they had given me when I arrived. I made off down the steep road towards Enniskerry, but I avoided passing through that village by taking a road that passed behind the village street which it rejoined a little beyond the far end of the village. I took the road by the Protestant church towards Bray. Where this joins the Wicklow road I turned towards Kilmacanogue for a few yards, and then turned into a lane which brought me into the Killarney road, from which I turned into the Boghall road, and so on to the Greystones road where I

179

turned in the direction of Bray. Before one reaches Bray there is the Putland road which joins one end of Novara Road in which part there were no houses at that time. Thus I could reach the end of the little street where I lived whence a few steps took me to my house. In all this walk I had not passed a soul or a vehicle on the road.

My wife was astounded when she saw me at the door which she opened. 'Why did you come here?' she asked. She had received word that day from the priests with whom I had spent the Saturday night, that I was safe. They probably thought that I was still in the house where they had sent me, or that I had gone from there to a safer place. She had also heard that certain friends would make arrangements for me to get off to America dressed as a priest, and now it seemed that with an utter disregard of safety I had insisted on coming home where I was bound to be captured. I hastily told her that I had come to that house because as far as my experience had gone it was the only place where I should be allowed to stay.

Shaw Letters

The Cuan,
Ventry,
Dingle,
Co. Kerry.
28th November, 1914.

Dear Mr. Shaw,

I was Mabel McConnell when I took Miss Gilmore's place with you for two or three months some years ago; I wonder if you remember me? I hope you do; I have very pleasant memories of my time with you and of your and Mrs. Shaw's kindness to me. I am married now and have a couple of youngsters, sons; the younger numbers his years in months only so far. Knowing how sorely tried you are in that respect, I will begin by telling you I am not writing to ask any personal favour of you. I want to call your attention to the campaign that is going on against the National Press of Ireland, the only truthful Press we have. Will you look over the papers I send you under another cover and take the matter up if it appeals to you. And do please let it appeal. I am sending you a couple of copies of *Ireland*, the recently launched daily which you will see compares most favourably with any London paper as mental food for supposedly, intelligent folk at this time; *Sinn Fein*, which is always worth reading; *The Irish Volunteer* and *The Irish Worker*. The latter, whilst sound on the national principle, is the only one which does not maintain a fairly high level of journalism, but you knowing the English Socialist papers will be able to allow for that. James Connelly is a straight thinker and a good writer at any rate.

Please don't put them aside even if you are busy at present but as an Irishman and as a recognised advocate of truth and liberty look

them over and I think the result will be that no matter what your
opinion as to the part Ireland should take in this war, you will raise
your very forcible voice in defence of a free Press for Ireland. I have
directed the Offices of the papers I am sending, and of *Irish Freedom*,
my copy of which is lent, to send you the current numbers if they
are not all suppressed by then; don't think me too obstrusive, I
shouldn't bother you about anything personal but this is a vital
matter for Ireland and you alone of all the literary and public men in
England have come forward courageously and spoken out about the
war. I have read your pamphlet in *The New Statesman*; it is a fine
piece of work and makes me wish more than ever that you would
stop bothering about such a childish and vacuous people as the English and come right over here to work for *Ireland a Nation*; I would
like to see you moved by a flash of revelation to shake the dust of
England off your feet and to put yourself in touch with all that is
most advanced in Nationalism here, to work as Roger Casement is
doing to make Ireland a Nation before Europe. That is the destiny I
would arrange for you, to fight with pen, purse, and shall I say pike,
to carry out the alliteration: guns will likely be scarce anyway, for
Ireland; has the great adventure no appeal for you?

If it has not, will you at least make a stand for the right of your
fellow countrymen and women to have a Press suited to their
mentality and in accordance with their national feelings and not a
vapid, atrocity mongering, 'Long Way to Tipperary' Press foisted on
them. Why shouldn't we speak out against recruiting and tell England plainly to use her own three million odd unmarried men of
fighting age before she asks us for our few hundred thousand to go
and be slaughtered like pigs in the Chicago stockyards? Ireland
wasn't asked if she wanted war and she has no enmity to Germany
nor any hope of getting share of the increased trade that England is
licking her lips for; we have no aspirations in common with the
English nation and how in the name of goodness can we have a
common Press? And we are more than a little indignant at the picture of us she is drawing for Europe, a slave race licking the hand
that chastises. And that the calumnies on men who have no thought
but Ireland, no interests but hers to serve; to spread the lie that they
are German spies and living on German gold! Of course, everyone
knows that the stories are lies, the same thing is said of South Africa
and of Egypt but what a nation! Unable to conceive of any but an

Englishman being moved by pure motives! I need not tell you that
there is no Nationalist in Ireland who is in receipt of German pay;
if any Irish nationalist was out for cash he could get it nearer at hand
by betraying his country to England as numbers of the Freeman staff
have done. Nor are the national papers circulated in motor cars, presumably German owned, in the West of Ireland. They are as here
stocked in the ordinary newsagents and are eagerly awaited in every
village and district in Ireland and are passed from house to house.
German money may reach Ireland; any German in the United States
is I presume free, as he ought to be, to subscribe to any fund that is
being raised there for Irish causes, but anyone who knows the
chronic poverty of Irish-Ireland treasuries will see that they have not
availed themselves of this very largely; now, as always, Irish people
keep their own organisations alive.

I suppose you know something of the real state of Ireland apart
from the stuff that the Parliamentary Party have published in their
subsidised Press? Redmond is dead as a doornail in Ireland, I don't
say this because he is a political opponent of the men I stand by; it is
an absolute fact and any person familiar with Ireland at the moment,
and honest, would tell you so; the country was more advanced
nationally than he knew—than anyone knew—even the strongest
separatist leaders—and he has sickened it. He still has a strong following, strong on paper and in sending paper resolutions to the Press,
but the Irish volunteers are the only real force, Redmond's are dum-
mies in almost every place and Redmond has now round him every
corrupt force in Ireland, Hibernianism, the rottenest of the priests
and gombeen men, the toadies and Shoneens, but every bit of brain
and spirit is on the side of Ireland a Nation. We hear the same reports
from every part where we have friends; the people are far sounder
than anyone believed, not only have they scouted recruiting—as one
old farmer here said to my husband the other day, he wouldn't send
his dog to fight for England—but they have shrewdly sized up the
Home Rule Bill and are quite unconcerned as to whether we ever
get that impotent measure or not. I need not tell you that Redmond
has undoubtedly a following still and has many good men among it
who are obsessed by the Irish reverence for a 'Leader', but they won't
subscribe to the recruiting plank in his platform and have their own
very decided opinions about this war. The thing that keeps their
allegiance is that they credit Redmond the honest Imperialist with

separatist aspirations for the eventual triumph of which he is throwing dust in the eyes of the English. That is a very common belief where he isn't discarded entirely.

You may be an Imperialist yourself but you will hardly expect a whole nation to like the doctrine being forced upon them instead of the dreams of nationhood they received from the generations that are gone, and you will not believe that the crushing of a few of the pages that express our ideas (there are some local papers too and others will rise if they are suppressed) will be conducive to peace in Ireland.

I am bringing up my small son with the sound traditional hatred of England and all her ways—you should just hear him say Sasanach, the concentrated hate in his voice is worthy of Drury Lane—and I don't care whether the *Daily News* lifts hands of horror or not at the ungodly sight. By the way, the youngster speaks Irish as his native tongue; that is why we came to live here in one of the Irish speaking districts where everyone talks it; of that I know you won't approve but you see I haven't changed a bit since I was with you.

I may say that it was on your advice I married; you urged the course on me frequently but I didn't carry out your advice entirely, for you always counselled a wealthy union whereas Desmond is a candidate for honours in your own profession of letters and so far we have not been crushed by weight of worldly wealth. You have been within sight of our house here though you must long ago have forgotten it; we heard the first day we arrived in Dingle that you have once stayed there the night and had motored round Slea Head. Well we live on the far side of Ventry bay, a mile or so off the Slea Head road, on a little peninsula out in the sea and far from neighbours. We have a disused coastguard station but can hardly expect to live in it undisturbed this winter for my husband is guilty of the awful crime of preaching nationalism in these parts and cannot move on that account without a policeman at his heels so we do not know at what moment we may become undesirable tenants. Unfortunately, we have the place on a six months' lease only; they would not sell it to us. If you motor round here again you would look me up, wouldn't you? It would give me such pleasure.

Police persecution is very prevalent in Ireland just now; there have been quite a number of cases too of young men in Government employ being dismissed summarily with no reason given and several other Nationalista have been ordered out of certain counties, while a girl in a Kerry town, Kilgarvin, was arrested and tried illegally for giving a man an anti-recruiting pamphlet. So you see things are decidedly unpleasant already; what will happen if the German fleet gives the English a hiding is only to be guessed—this is the 'Union of Hearts' that all Europe hears of.

Forgive my prolixity and will you remember me to Mrs. Shaw if she recalls me? And Greetings to Miss Gilmore, Respects to yourself,

From

Yours very sincerely,

P.S. I didn't tell you that I did some work for George Moore after I left you, before my marriage three years and a half ago.

Ayot St. Lawrence,
Welwyn, Herts.
1st December, 1914.

My dear Mabel,

You are just a day after the fair: I have already taken action. I do not want Prussia to win this game: I am convinced that it is the interest of all of us to shew that a quite casual army of poor English, Irish and Scotch civilians, without any previous military training or tradition, picked up for the occasion on the nod, can knock the stuffing out of the Prussian military machine, and thus not only to discredit the jackboot theory of society, but convince the Bavarian and the easygoing, friendly south German generally that he would have had just as good a chance in the field if he had lived happily and naturally as he has now after submitting to a Prussian tyranny which he loathes, and which he stood solely because he had been assured that in that way only could he be saved from destruction by France and the other enemies of his country, notably perfidious Albion.

Also, I want to establish the assumption that Ireland is on the Republican side, and on the democratic side: which in this war means the side of France against Prussia. I admit that Russia introduces an unlucky complication; but its a long long way to Petrograd, and France is our old ally and next door neighbour.

Consequently I have written to the Irish papers to the above effect generally, with the intention of setting back the pro-German propaganda in Ireland, and suggesting to the British Government that there are more tactful ways of encouraging recruiting than suppressing the Nationalist papers.

I have not yet seen the papers you sent me, as they are at Adelphi Terrace and have not been sent on with the letters. I am going up to town this evening and shall study them with interest, as *The Times* here has been full of quotations from the *Irish Volunteer*.

Your marriage was a most selfish and unreasonable proceeding, because Judy Gilmore got married and left me without a secretary. Naturally I went in search of you, and could learn nothing except that you were married and living somewhere in the south with sixteen children. If Judy had not found a Scotch lady for me, I should have been completely stranded through your desertion. I am sorry you did not think me as amusing as FitzGerald. Who is FitzGerald anyhow, that he should have my secretary?

As an Ulsterwoman, you must be aware that if you bring up your son to hate anyone except a Papist, you will go to hell. Just you see what I have said in my letter to the Irish Press about people who have no positive nationality and are only anti-English instead of being Irish. You must be a wicked devil to load a child's innocent soul with a burden of old hatreds and rancours that Ireland is sick of. When Ireland no longer fears England, she will no longer hate her. How are we ever to discover our sins (and a black thick lot they are) if we keep our eyes always on the sins of our neighbors? You make that boy a good International Socialist—a good Catholic, in fact, in the true sense—and make him understand that the English are far more oppressed than any folk he has ever seen in Ireland by the same forces that have oppressed Ireland in the past. And remind him that all the oppressors of Ireland have been Irishmen, damn them! You see what comes of deserting me and seeing the world from Slea Head. By the way, teach that Boy any classical languages or modern Volapuks or Esperantos you like to torment him with; but don't forget to teach him that he who is master of the English language is master of the world. We Irish ought to know that, as we have done so much to forge the weapon to its finest temper. However, he will find out all this for himself. Nothing educates a man like the desire to free himself by proving that everything his parents say is wrong.

I did not, Madam, stay a night in Dingle. I stayed for one midday meal, and my wife remembers that meal still. I went round the peninsula and put up in Tralee, where I at last heard one person speak with the old Kerry accent instead of with the dialect of the Dublin elementary school teacher. And strange to say, that person was a small boy selling newspapers. I will certainly call on you next time to see whether you have kept your good looks. The magic of Ireland is very strong for me when I see a beehive dwelling. Did you ever make the pilgramage to Skelling Michael? If not, you have not yet seen Ireland.

I was on the point of mentioning to the British public the other day that Sir Roger Casement was perfectly in order in exercising our inalienable right as a nation to consult any other nation as to our future or present or past relations; but I didn't quite know what his credentials were; and in this war emergency I did not want to start more hares than I could help.

As to devoting myself to Ireland, I doubt whether Ireland would at all appreciate my services. The place is too small for me. The earth and the fullness thereof are good enough for me. Russell and Sir Horace Plunkett and you can look after local affairs; but Ireland must must have an ambassador in the great world; so I am better as I am. You may possibly remember also that I am an elderly gentleman of $58\frac{1}{2}$, and that my bolt is shot.

This letter is not being typed by the Scotch lady. I am slamming through it myself at a frightful rate, with oceans of work howling to be done; and I cannot attempt to answer your letter properly. It is the only letter I have answered at all for years except under pressure of absolute necessity. But your letter has given me great pleasure personally, and is very interesting as well; so if you will condescend to join the ranks of those friends of mine who can stand writing to me and never getting an answer oftener than every five years or so, I can at least assure you that your letters will never be unwelcome, and that the Scotch lady (Miss Elder) shall have instructions that they are to be privileged communications. She has a soulless way of putting letters from ladies into the waste paper basket when they run to more than thirty pages and are directed to my eternal salvation or breathe a hopeless adoration for my person under misapprehensions as to my age and the color of my hair. But you shall write 3000000000000000000000000000000000000000000000000000000000000000 pages if you like; and they shall all be read from beginning to end

In furious haste, ever and a day,
G. Bernard Shaw.

The Cuan,
Ventry,
Dingle.
Friday evening.

Dear Mr. Shaw,

Your friendliest of letters received today with much pleasure: it was more than good of you to type it yourself.

I haven't finished with you yet and mean to write you again tomorrow if you can stand it to enlighten you on a few points in the present situation in Ireland upon which I can't help thinking you a bit hazy. Notably that we are all out and out Republicans but mean to make a shot for that Republic by a shorter cut than you suggest.

In the meantime I send a couple of *Ireland*'s and *Irish Freedom*, perhaps the last issue. I should be very glad on that account if you would get your secretary to return the copy when you have finished with it. In *Ireland* I have marked the paragraphs that give the history of the measures so far adopted towards suppression. There are answers to you too; the one in Thursday's issue makes some good points.

I would be writing you all I had to say in this instead of taking up your time on several occasions but we live nine long miles from Dingle and are dependent on our neighbour's donkey cart for provisions; in weather like this when Atlantic gales sweep over the peninsula no one . . . and with the children safely in bed, I must bake.

Cuan,
Ventry,
Dingle,
Co. Kerry.
December 7th, 1914.

Dear Mr. Shaw,

You will have seen all about the suppression of the Irish Nationalist Press—as distinguished from the Irish Imperialist Press, represented by the *Freeman*, *Independent*, *Cork Examiner*, etc. I fear all the National papers have gone under owing to the attack on the printers. Arthur Griffith had intended to bring out a new paper this week, *Nationality*, in lieu of the suppressed *Sinn Fein*, but I suppose that he can't now for lack of a printer. Eoin MacNeill, President of the

Irish Volunteers took over the *Irish Volunteer* this week. It was not the official organ before. But it is said to have been seized in Cork, so we shall hardly have another issue. I enclose circular which came in place of the defunct *Ireland* to-day. There are other papers of the same views as the *Leader*, and a couple of little volunteer papers in Cork, and some local weeklies, *Kerryman*, *Mayo News* and, I think, the *Enniscorthy Echo*; there may be a few others that I don't know of, but all these will have to hide their principles if they wish to live. *The Leader* has been very strongly national lately, but since the editor, Moran, is a man of recognised business ability and made a good living out of it, the only editor of a national paper who did, it will likely moderate its views considerably now that the Government have threatened it. It is a very pro-Catholic paper, popularly believed to circulate solely among Protestants and priests. It has always plenty of advertisements.

It is obvious that the country has gone pretty strongly pro-German, or at the best neutral, when all these papers existed at once; there has never been such a number of extreme national papers in Ireland before.

This suppression of the Press is only the first step I think; disarmament may come next and, of course, the prosecution and policy persecution of known nationalists will increase rather than decrease. It is probable that seeing how completely the country has gone pro-German, the Government have decided that it is necessary to risk unpopularity in America and the exposure before Europe of the true situation in Ireland, and to dragoon us into such a state of impotence that we should be too weak to take our opportunity should it come. They may even contemplate provoking a premature rising in Ireland as they did in '98, but it is to be hoped that we will have the sense to bide our own time now and not be provoked into striking at an hour of England's choosing. Of course, to expect success from any physical force movement unless with the help of Germany would be madness just now when England has been careful to redouble the garrison in Ireland; only a defeat of the British fleet, followed by a landing in Ireland of the Germans could give us our opportunity. Naturally, people speak little of these things, but the hope is in the air and one thing is very certain—if the Germans ever do land in Ireland, no one but the coastguards will strike a blow; even if they land among the hottest Redmondites, there will be no fight put up. I presume they won't choose to land in Ulster.

I want to make very clear to you that when I say this, neither Desmond nor I hold any official position in National affairs and we are far from Dublin, the storm centre of Nationalism. But Ireland is rather like an Eastern country; one can feel its national pulse in the remotest corners, and I should be prepared to stake a good deal on the statement that the majority of Ireland outside of Ulster is pro-German in this war. For sentimental reasons, hatred of England and love of a brave fighter, she necessarily is on Germany's side, and of course for the common sense reason that Germany holds the potentiality of nationhood for us. Since the war started Ireland has put aside the shabby little dream of paper freedom that was all Redmond could get from England and has seen a larger vision. Casement's action has, of course, had an inestimable effect; we have now an ambassador abroad and there is no Kerry farmer or labourer who hearing that story, does not instantly grasp something of what it means. We are a nation now before the world and have a new self-respect on that account. I wish you had written to the Press to the effect that such an embassy was our inalienable right as a nation. I shall bear in mind that you do think Ireland a nation—that involves other things from you.

I am writing freely to you on what I think to be the hope of Ireland today knowing not at all if that hope will appeal to you, though I imagine that if your Nationalist sympathies are not sufficiently strong to move you, your Republic ones may. Whatever you feel about it I am very anxious to avoid being the innocent cause of bringing trouble on the men who are working for Irish Nationalism at the moment, or of hastening the action of the Government or by giving you material to write something which might turn out to be indiscreet and the effects of which you could not guess. I know the last thing you would want to engage in, no matter how you might be opposed to the present aims of Irish Nationalists, would be felon setting. That is one reason why I am sorry you wrote that letter to the Freeman, apart from its content; for the Freeman has been busily engaged in felon setting recently. Besides it has been bought body and soul by Lady Aberdeen and those she serves, not the first time by many in its shady career that such a transaction has taken place, and the Staff and paper, nicely disinfected so as to cause no danger to her

Ladyship's person, have been neatly stowed away in her pocket. No decent Irish men or women give a fig for it; you should hear it disdussed by decent farmers.

What is wanted now is for someone to clear the air by asserting Ireland's right if she doesn't like the bone which England offers, and which she has a strong suspicion England intends to snatch away and fling to hungry Carson, to try and secure a fuller meal from Germany if that country is enabled by circumstances to offer it. Nobody else but you could to it and keep out of prison and you may not see your way to. But at any rate you can be counted on, can't you, to keep a strict watch on England for acts of injustice or oppression beyond the ordinary and to publish them to America and Europe. If you don't act as a big policeman on behalf of your country when you see the bullies worrying the life out of her, you aren't the man I take you for.

I wish you would impose on yourself a rule to judge everything first as an Irishman. You wouldn't be bothering about Prussian Militarism then; to an Irishman it is six of one and half a dozen of the other, with the balance down against England who spends 70 odd millions on her Army and Navy to Germany's 59 millions. And Prussian militarism, in as far as it exists at all, outside the imagination of the English newspaper man, isn't half so galling I am sure as that we endure it in the south of Ireland under the iron heel of the R.I.C. I'll bet you anything too that if England wins this war she will institute conscription in spite of all you may say; a victorious military party will make short work of your arguments. As for Democracy, surely that would forge ahead in Europe best with England, the home of Capitalism, smashed up? I wouldn't give much for the freedom of the English democracy after this war if England wins, with their teeth drawn by taxation and high prices, their hands and feet bound by all the philanthropy that has been thrust upon them in the shape of this fund and that fund—they will be just in the position for the final gagging that the Cursons and Sir William Bulls have been shrieking for for years. However, it isn't our business—we have ourselves to think of; Ireland is pretty sick of having sentimental courses of chivalry and self-sacrifice pointed out to her to follow, while other nations frankly—except of course England, which never confesses it—follow the good old aim of grab. We know that if England wins we will have to face coercion as bad as any in penal days;

once she is free of the German menace she won't spare us. This might have seemed a far fetched idea a few months ago, but so would the laws we are living under now have been thought.

I believe that this letter of mine, if read by the authorities, would land me in penal servitude or something like that, if it wasn't that you are a person of such importance that even this humourless Government would hardly risk incurring the ridicule of Europe and America by hauling so insignificant a person as myself up for trying to subvert your allegiance.

Casement has every credential that an Irish ambassador requires, and I wish from the bottom of my heart that you had redeemed that letter of yours by making the reference to him you thought of making. Handsome, polished, charming, a man of the world, and a man of absolute integrity, of courage, and known in National circles as sound. But have you met him? If not, you must imagine a heroic figure from some old romance—a knight of the old times, tall, dark, romantically bearded, and in temperament and character in accordance with his appearance. Sane undoubtedly, in spite of Conan Doyle than whom—in spite of his Irish birth—there never was a more typical Broadbent. This act of Casement's is no sudden madness; I have known him as an extreme Nationalist for quite eight years—he was often in Belfast (he is a Ballycastle, Co. Antrim, man) on holidays from S. America and never concealed his views, and some years ago I met him in London, and again in Belfast last Xmas at the house of Francis Joseph Bigger, nephew of the Joe Bigger of Parnell's time. While acknowledging his charming manner and rich personality, I must say that he did not make a strong personal appeal to me, (not like yourself who I always tell people I characterise as the nicest man I ever met, when I am asked what you are like) owing to a lack of geniality in him, but that may be a great advantage to him if he is destined to play the part of Irish leader.

Redmond is undoubtedly discredited; he acted like a booby, if not worse. Even if he didn't do as I should have done that day war was declared—stand up in the British House of Commons—I wish I had had his opportunity—I am convinced Ireland would have rallied to him to a man—wouldn't your own back have straightened to read of it next day—he could at least have made terms. He will go down in history as the greatest traitor we have ever produced, unless his mental incapacity is taken into account and a more charitable judgment made on him for that reason. A British ever, he be, of course, but what is that to the chance he had of making his ——— as a statesman and a patriot.

Well I set out to tell you some things about Ireland I thought you didn't know, and I find I have mostly occupied myself in airing my opinions, but they are in the main those of the rest of Ireland and representative at least of the young men and women and of the . . . The old, the middle aged, are probably Redmond supporters—the products of the most barren period we've had in Ireland.

Though I won't let you or anyone bully me about Prussian militarism or anything else, I have an immense respect for your intellect and a great liking for your person, as you say is common with my sex. I shall write you sometime again if I think I have anything of interest to tell you about events in Ireland, and I should like to write to tell you something about the plans I have for my boys' education. You had a lot of advice to give me on the subject, and it is one to which I have devoted a good deal of thought.

By the way, I do want to ask you something. I met Sasha Kropotkin since the day she wrote her first article about Ferrer and found her charming, but is she qualified to write about the Russian army? Do the officers really take their men to picture palaces, and is the efficiency of the army increased thereby? Or is it Democracy that gains? If the officers were to accept invitations from their men to accompany them to your plays I could see the democratic bearings of it.

Amn't I a divil for spinning out a letter? I do hope I haven't bored you to wishing you hadn't replied to my last screed.

P.S. I wonder would you think me too indescribably rude after pitching these things at you unasked—if I asked you to get your Secretary to make me a parcel of all those Irish papers, if you don't want them, and send them back. They must be sent as a parcel to reach Nationalists at all. We are awful misers about our Irish papers which we keep for reference. Both of us have piles for years back and shall value them all the more now there are no more.

Ayot St. Lawrence,
Welwyn,
Herts.
12th & 13th December 1914.

My dear Mabel,

This won't do at all: it belongs to a bygone slavery, and may plunge us back into it.

All the hopes of the Unionists have been revived by the pro-German folly in Ireland. They have never given up the hope that they can, by military mutiny if necessary, prevent the Act being carried out. Their hopes fell badly when the Bill was passed. They fell lower when Redmond offered the Nationalists of Ireland for service against Germany. Then this folly of pro-Germanism, this recrudescence of the Clan na Gael suddenly shewed them a way out. They saw that if the Irish could once be tempted to turn against England in the war, Home rule would be repealed before it had ever been put into action. And they are quite right. Only throw Ireland on the side of Prussia in this war, and the weary labor of nearly fifty years will be wiped out at a stroke. All the democracies of the world will spew us out of their mouths as an incorrigible people, fighting for negro slavery in the American Civil War, and fighting for the devastators of Belgium and the destroyers of human happiness and liberty by the very system of military despotism that has crushed ourselves.

If you have one atom of sense left—if the little view from Dingle has not made you forget the whole great political horizon of Europe —you will try to make Ireland resound with anti-Prussianism until the end of the war. If the Germans tried an invasion through Ireland, it would be Ireland's business and Ireland's opportunity to make as desperate a stand to delay them, at whatever cost in murder and destruction, as Belgium.

I hope most Irishmen have the sense to see this; but if not, then Ireland's cause is hopeless. It will always be possible for any knave or fool to provoke Ireland to cut her own throat by some silly appeal to her hatred of England, or her inveterate cheap derision of any leaders she can find.

Horace Plunkett is about the ablest, honestest and whitest man in practical politics at present. Nobody in Ireland or in England or Scotland for that matter, can touch his record. He has succeeded in attaching to himself A.E., who is the greatest and most patriotic journalist in Ireland. They have done things, and done the right things, and stuck to doing them through good and evil report. And you, like a true Irishwoman, think nothing of them because they are not good enough for you. A co-operative dairy leaves you cold; a romantic expedition to Berlin by a knight errant who should have gone to offer France or Belgium the last drop of our blood delights you. I prefer the co-operative dairy and the knight errant who transfixes the giant instead of the distressed damsel.

Redmond may not be your ideal; but he is big enough to have done the right thing on this not very difficult occasion. In Ireland we have always suffered from a plague of clever fools always saying the wrong thing in the most skilful way. When you get a stupid man who says the right thing with rhetoric enough to make himself listened to, be thankful for him, and stand by him until you have somebody better to put in his place.

Now, having abused you sufficiently for amusing yourself with the affairs of Ireland instead of working at them, let me say one or two more general things. The day of small nations is past; indeed, except for nations still denied self-government, nationalism is a dead horse: and even the subject nations like Ireland must never forget that the moment they gain home rule, the horse will drop down under them and reveal, by a sudden and horrible decomposition, that he has been dead for years. Only as a member of a great commonwealth is there any future for us. We are a wretched little clod, broken off a bigger clod, broken off the west end of Europe, full of extraordinarily beautiful but damnably barren places, with a strange climate that degrades base people hideously and clears the souls of noble people wonderfully. We are capable of taking a very high degree of training; in fact, we are rather dangerous without it. We have the enormous advantage of exceptional literary power and a language which puts us into communication with a fifth of the human race. We are not rich enough to become fatheaded and demoralized like our bigger neighbors. In short, we shall be either a very highly civilized people or nothing; and this means that we should carefully preserve our relations with the large countries. There are two main reasons for this. i. Our own market for ideas (that, for books) is so small that only by keeping hold of the whole English speaking market can Irishmen obtain publication for literary work of the highest class. ii. Only through pooling our resources with Great Britain can we profit by the comparative cheapness and convenience of international organisation of modern international services (postal and so forth) or economise the expense of a fleet and army.

Now if Sinn Fein means that we are to decide and arrange all this for ourselves instead of having it arranged for us by others, then more power to Sinn Fein's elbow. But if S.F. means that we are to turn back and shrink into a little village community with a sham wide language that nobody in the world speaks, and do nothing but wonder how much longer the turf will last in Donegal, then the proper place for Sinn Fein is the ashpit. All that side of the Irish movement is not Irish; it was invented in Bedford Park, London, W.

Perhaps a greater danger is our poisonous gift of scorn and snobbery, which inclines us so dangerously towards old oligarchies, like the southern planters of America, and even towards such a machine-made modern imitation of Marlborough's England and Louis the fourteenth's France as the Prussian militarist State. We imagine we are democratic because we are rebellious; but when we have no longer any foreign tyranny to rebel against we may discover that we have yet to learn the A B C of democracy.

This is Sunday morning, so I cannot send your papers back today; but they are safe and shall be sent presently. I must break off now, having written far too much; but I want to rub your eyes for you and waken you up. Ireland is your plaything at present, because you are an educated woman trying to live the life of a peasant. You have put yourself out of reach of Beethoven and the orchestra; so I suppose you must have something to play with. But you shan't play with ME, madam; and with that I beg to subscribe myself.

Yours most obedient
G. Bernard Shaw.

10 Adelphi Terrace,
London, W.C.
29th Januray, 1915.

My dear Mabel,

All this is very distressing; and it all comes of your not doing what

I tell you. What do you expect the authorities to do? Here we are engaged in a most appalling war. At any moment a bomb may drop on me from a German aeroplane and finish this letter abruptly. At any moment any coast town on the east of England or the west of Ireland may find sixteen inch shells—Protestant, Prussian, intensely anti-Irish shells—dropping into it from German battle cruisers. And this is the moment that you, living in a western coastguard station, select to announce that you are the implacable enemy of England and France and Belgium, and, by implication, an enthusiastic wisher of success to German armies. I ask you again, what do you expect any unfortunate Government to do under such circumstances? Surely not to leave you in the western coastguard station with all its possibilities of signalling to your friend the enemy? All they have done to you is to transfer you to the east coast without denying you the benefit of sea air. What would you have done if *you* had been the Government and the coastguard station in Kerry had been occupied by a violent Unionist with a hostile fleet in the offing? Are you quite sure that your sense of injustice does not arise from the fact that you really have been playing at Irish patriotism, and that what seems to you so unjust is the terrible disproportion between your play and the earnest of the Government and of the Germans. You ask me if I think it a game to have to separate from your babies at very short notice; to be turned out of your house; and to be shadowed here, there and everywhere by employees of the British Government. Of course, it is not a game; they do it because they took you seriously as their enemy; and under those circumstances you can hardly claim that they could have done less. They could have let you entirely alone only on the assumption that you were of no account whatever, and that you did not really dislike them.

You really must not be an Impossibilist. I know, of course, that is is very little use talking to a born Orangewoman who is also a bit of a spoilt beauty; but I have some pity for those unfortunate babies, and some masculine sympathy with Desmond, whose head you are knocking against a stone wall. In Ireland the enormous majority of the population, north and south, orange and green, know perfectly well that we have got to see the English and the French through this fight with Prussia. They may not all believe, as I do, that there is no future for small and poor independent states of the size and means of Ireland, and that only in such a position as is occupied by any one of the United States of America can she enjoy either real freedom or real power; but at all events none of them believe that she would be better off in the position of Posen than she is at present. Therefore, in Ireland you are standing out against both Ireland and England; and under martial law this is bound to get you and yours into trouble quite uselessly. If you are going on with it, there is nothing for it but America, where the American Gaels will welcome you with open arms. But I had much rather you rallied to my banner, which is your proper and natural place as an Irishwoman.

At worst, you can always wreak your political indignation on me and not on the authorities until the war is over. I positively forbid you to get yourself into trouble out of mere devilment. Just look round the world and see what patriotism is reducing men to do at the present time; and then tell me to my face, if you dare, that there is not quite enough of it already.

Yours sincerely,
G. Bernard Shaw.

Index

Aberdeen, Lady, 189
Abbey Theatre, 22
Anglo-Irish Literary Movement, 3

Biggar, Francis Joseph, 31, 192
Biggar, Joseph, 192
Birrell, Augustine, 85
Blythe, Ernest, 17–64, 69–71, 77, 78, 95, 109–12, 117, 120
Brugha, Cathal, 29, 67, 68, 123
Bull, Sir William, 191

Carson, Edward, 191
Casement, Sir Roger, 31, 182, 187, 190, 192
Ceannt, Eamonn, 62, 113
'Claidheamh Soluis', 24–7
Clan na Gael, 194
Clarke, Thomas, 132, 133, 148, 149, 152
Collins, Michael, 144
Conan Doyle, Sir Arthur, 192
Connolly, James, 31, 132, 133, 148, 181
Conroy, — 105

Cork Examiner, 188
Cotton, Alf, 50, 51
Curragh Mutiny, 38
Curzon, Lord, 191

Daily News, 183
Deichmann, Hans Christian, 101–4
De Valera, Eamonn, 114
Dillon, John, 42
Downey, Peggy, 143, 144, 154, 159

Enniscorthy Echo, 189

Fenianism, 35
Fianna Fail, 62
FitzGerald, Mabel, 64, 69, 91, 108, 115, 117–19, 121, 125, 129, 130, 138, 180
Flower, Robin, 23
Freeman's Journal, 188, 190

Gaelic League, 18, 23, 27
Gavan Duffy, Louise, 150, 155, 156, 159

Gilmore, Judy, 181, 185, 186
Griffith, Arthur, 2–4, 19, 21, 23, 29, 63, 72, 73

Hobson, Bulmer, 26, 29, 51, 70, 113–25, 128, 148, 174, 175
Home Rule, 4, 5, 23–7, 32–4, 38, 39, 41, 56, 183
Hulme, T. E., 21

IRB, 26, 27, 29, 41, 50, 51, 63, 64, 71, 73, 86, 110
Ireland, 181, 188, 189
Irish Freedom, 182, 188
Irish Independent, 188
Irish Party, 4, 23, 28, 33, 34, 37, 40, 54, 183
Irish Volunteer, 181, 186, 189
Irish Worker, 181

Joachim, Prince, 141

Kelly, Alderman Tom, 30
Kerryman, 189
Kropotkin, Sasha, 193

Larkin, James, 135
Leader, 189
Lester, Sean, 30
Long, Willie, 9, 11, 13, 16

McCabe, Alec, 105
MacAlister, Prof., 8
McCann, Pierce, 23
McDermott, 50, 91, 151, 154
McDonagh, 79, 80, 113, 114
MacNeill, Prof. Eoin, 26–9, 57, 121, 123, 125–9, 164, 174, 175, 188

Marstrander, Carl, 8
Mayo News, 189
Mellowes, Liam, 109, 111
Moore, George, 185
Moran, —, 189
Mullen, Billy, 51

Nationality, 188
Nationalist Party, *see* Irish Party
National Volunteers, 54, 122
New Statesman, 182

O'Casey, Sean, 21
O'Connell, Daniel, 42
O'Criomhthain, Tomas, 8
O'Duffy, Eimar, 82, 88, 89
Oglaigh na hEireann, 62
O'Kane, Michael, 51
O'Rahilly, Madame, 127, 129
O'Rahilly, Michael (The O'Rahilly), 21–9, 40–2, 47, 57, 62, 64, 85, 86, 96, 108–12, 116–17, 121, 123, 124, 126, 130–3, 136–9, 145, 152, 154, 155, 164, 165

Parliamentary Party, *see* Irish Party
Parnell, Charles, 35
Pearse, Mrs., 172
Pearse, Patrick, 113, 118, 130, 132–44, 148, 154
Plunkett, Sir Horace, 187, 193, 195
Plunkett, Joseph, 136, 138–43, 149
Pockmeyer, —, 104
Pound, Ezra, 21

Redmond, John, 4, 35, 37, 41, 46, 47, 53, 183, 190, 192, 195

Russell, George (AE), 187, 193, 195

Shaw, George Bernard, 64, 181, *et seq.*

Shaw, Mrs. George Bernard, 181, 185

Sinn Fein, 181, 188

Stack, Austin, 50, 51, 67

Talbot-Crosbie, —, 36, 37, 53

Thomas, Edward, 22

'Times', 186

Ulster Volunteers, 25-7, 38, 39, 41

Yeats, W. B., 3

143736